WHAT'S NEXT FOR ORGANIZED LABOR?

REPORT OF THE CENTURY FOUNDATION
TASK FORCE ON THE FUTURE OF UNIONS

WHAT'S NEXT FOR ORGANIZED LABOR?

with a background paper by
NELSON LICHTENSTEIN

1999 ◆ THE CENTURY FOUNDATION PRESS ◆ NEW YORK

The Century Foundation, formerly the Twentieth Century Fund, sponsors and supervises timely analyses of economic policy, foreign affairs, and domestic political issues. Not-for-profit and nonpartisan, it was founded in 1919 and endowed by Edward A. Filene.

LIBRARY OF CONGRESS CATALOGING-IN-PUBLICATION DATA

What's next for organized labor?: the report of The Century Foundation Task Force on the Future of Unions.
    p. cm.
    "With background paper by Nelson Lichtenstein."
    Includes index.
    ISBN 0-87078-418-8
    1. Labor--United States--Forecasting. 2. Labor policy--United States. 3. Trade-unions--United States. 4. Industrial relations--United States. I. Lichtenstein, Nelson. II. Century Foundation Task Force on the Future of Unions.
    HD8072.5.R458 1998
    331.8'0973--dc21   98-20418
                                                   CIP

Cover Design: Claude Goodwin

Manufactured in the United States of America.

GCIU

FOREWORD

Unions have been losing ground in the United States since the mid-1950s, and the evidence of their decline is widespread. In the political arena, for example, the bashing of labor unions has become a staple of many campaigns, which may be the surest evidence of the current perceived weakness of organized labor. The advocacy of privatization in the public sector, as well, is often no more than a thinly disguised effort to circumvent existing union agreements. For unions at century's end, the underlying statistics are grim: since the 1950s, when it topped out at about 35 percent, union membership has declined to about 14 percent of the workforce. Moreover, a series of statutes and court decisions has made it more difficult for unions to win representation fights with hostile companies. Oddly, unions have been losing ground not because average U.S. workers have been doing better. Indeed, until very recently, even the current, historically exceptional economic expansion was not lifting inflation-adjusted income levels for hourly-wage employees. In fact, their incomes had been nearly stagnant for more than two decades. The basic case for organization—a fair share of the growing pie for workers—seems obvious, the reasons for the decline in union membership less so.

In this context, we saw an opportunity to shed light on a topic of interest to The Century Foundation since the Great Depression. Our founder, Edward A. Filene, set up a special committee on labor that helped to draft legislative recommendations strengthening collective bargaining rights. Even in the postwar economy, we continued to examine the issues facing workers in the United States.

Our interest in worker-related issues has been consistent, and a few years ago, we convened a task force on the future of unions. Our hope was that gathering a diverse group of prominent Americans who care about labor would generate ideas that might revitalize the movement to the benefit of the nonunionized, low- and middle-income workers who have been losing economic ground. Questions and concerns similar to ours among union members themselves had a great deal to do with the replacement in 1996 of long-standing AFL-CIO leadership with a new team headed by John Sweeney.

Over a two-year period, many ideas were explored in a series of meetings chaired by former Ohio governor Richard Celeste. By the time Governor Celeste had to relinquish his task force responsibilities to become U.S. ambassador to India, the suggestions members offered spanned a range of topics. Some argued that labor's first priority ought to be to strengthen its organizing efforts through a variety of tactics. Others felt that the bleeding was unlikely to stop until antiquated labor laws were transformed to increase the probability that workers would vote in favor of unionizing. The failure of the Dunlop Commission earlier in the 1990s to bring about labor law reform convinced other members that labor's energy would be better expended on political causes that could broadly benefit workers, nonunionized as well as unionized. And a minority of task force members believed that efforts to organize workers outside of traditional unions held the most promise for strengthening the clout of large numbers of employees.

One major point of consensus emerged: the decline of the labor movement has imposed serious economic and social costs on the nation. The task force agreed that nonunionized as well as unionized workers, and the country as a whole, would be better off if that decline could be reversed. They agreed that the claim that America's low level of unionization relative to other countries has enabled it to achieve greater economic growth and lower unemployment overlooks the wide gaps in household earnings, health insurance, and pension coverage between the nation's haves and have-nots. Moreover, the members concurred that the weakness of labor unions contributed to the dramatic widening of those gaps in recent years. The task force report may convince many who are agnostic about organized labor, or even hostile toward it, to question whether the demise of unions would be good for the country.

Still, perhaps reflecting the vexing nature of the problems confronting labor, the task force was unable to reach a consensus about what the labor movement ought to do to reverse its fortunes. The range of opinions conveyed in this report confirms the fact that the challenge facing organized labor is so enormous that no silver bullet is likely to make a major dent in the problem. Because the labor force is growing while some current union members are retiring, unions need to add about 300,000 new members a year just to retain their current share of the workforce. Even though organizing rates have improved in the past couple of years, the unionized portion of the labor force still has declined. Compounding that grim math is the unpopularity of unions in areas of the country where job growth is high and the immense political clout of business in Congress.

Recognizing the headwinds against the labor movement, the members of the task force collectively advise it to pull out all the stops. Organize full throttle. Reclaim political issues that matter to all workers, not just union members. Continue to fight to modernize labor laws, even though that goal may be beyond the visible horizon. Although the task force members differed on how they would set priorities for these and other recommendations, the forcefulness of their conviction that a strong labor movement is good for the nation matches the urgency of the mission.

In the background paper to this report, University of Virginia historian Nelson Lichtenstein summarizes the story of organized labor's rise and fall. Weaving together the themes that began to emerge in the early decades of the century that would later evolve in ways that undermined the power of labor unions, Lichtenstein's analysis demonstrates why the decline has been so prolonged and inexorable. To a large extent, labor's problems have been a product of uncontrollable economic changes, most notably the diminishing share of workers in its manufacturing base. But the actions of labor and its leaders in the 1960s, 1970s, and 1980s often exacerbated those difficulties, alienating the movement from many of those who might have benefited from joining. Lichtenstein's lessons from the past helped to guide the task force's deliberations.

This project is one of many that The Century Foundation continues to sponsor related to widening economic inequality in the United States. James K. Galbraith's *Created Unequal: The Crisis in American Pay* and Robert Kuttner's *Everything for Sale: The Virtues and Limits of Markets* reinforce the view presented in this task force report that declining unionization contributed to greater inequality. MIT economist Paul Osterman's book *Securing Prosperity: The American Labor Market* explores transformations in the workplace, including the decline of unionization. Other authors exploring these themes for The Century Foundation include Jeffrey Madrick, Peter Diamond, Edward N. Wolff, Theda Skocpol, Simon Head, Jonas Pontusson, and Barry Bluestone (and the late Bennett Harrison).

We are particularly grateful to Richard Celeste, who led the group's discussions with energy and creativity. Drawing on his experience as governor of Ohio in wrestling with management-labor difficulties, Ambassador Celeste pressed the group to answer such difficult questions as what it would take for labor unions to appeal to a young software designer in Silicon Valley. Unfortunately, Ambassador Celeste's departure for India probably made a consensus on recommendations more difficult. All members are convinced that, if anyone could have forged an agreement, it would have been Dick Celeste.

We also want to thank Carol O'Cleireacain, who served as executive director of the task force and wrote important sections of the final report. The depth of her concern for, knowledge of, and insight into these issues made her invaluable.

Richard C. Leone, PRESIDENT
The Century Foundation
November 1999

CONTENTS

MEMBERS OF THE TASK FORCE

Zoë Baird
President, The John and Mary R. Markle Foundation

Betty Bednarczyk
International Secretary/Treasurer,
Service Employees International Union

Richard B. Freeman
Program Director, National Bureau of Economic Research, and
Ascherman Professor of Economics, Harvard University

Charles Heckscher
Professor, School of Management and Labor Relations,
Rutgers University

Calvin Hill
Consultant, Alexander & Associates

Lewis B. Kaden
Partner, Davis Polk & Wardwell

Eugene J. Keilin
Principal, Keilin & Co. LLC, and
KPS Special Situations Fund L.P.

Robert Kuttner
Founder and Co-editor, *The American Prospect*

Nelson Lichtenstein, *Background Paper Author*
Professor of History, University of Virginia

Lance E. Lindblom
Program Officer, Ford Foundation

Jay Mazur
President, Union of Needletrades, Industrial, and Textile
Employees (UNITE!)

Basil A. Paterson
Partner, Meyer, Suozzi, English & Klein, P.C.

Richard Ravitch
Principal, Ravitch, Rice & Company

Bruce Simon
Partner, Cohen, Weiss and Simon

David A. Smith
Director Public Policy, AFL-CIO

Bob Welsh
Executive Assistant to the President and Chief of Staff, AFL-
CIO

Carol O'Cleireacain, *Task Force Executive Director*
Senior Fellow, The Brookings Institution

REPORT OF THE TASK FORCE

Since the 1950s, union membership in the United States relative to the number of jobs has been in a free fall. After peaking at 35 percent of nonfarm payrolls in 1954, unionization steadily declined to 29 percent in 1964, 26 percent in 1973, and about 14 percent as it now stands. The number of individuals who belong to unions has fallen steadily in the past twenty years, from more than 22 million in the late 1970s to a little more than 16 million last year. Leaving out government employment, in 1997 union membership dropped below 10 percent of the private sector workforce for the first time since before World War II. Today, the frequency of union membership in the United States is lower than it is in any industrialized nation except France (where, however, unions bargain for entire industries, not only for their members).

In some quarters, especially corporate executive suites, the reaction to the continuous erosion of unions is an unambiguous "good riddance." The litany of complaints about unions is long and familiar: they hurt corporate profitability; they encourage confrontation and rigid work rules that undermine productivity; they rely excessively on painful, disruptive strikes that often benefit no one; and they behave politically like a special interest that places the concerns of members ahead of the needs of workers generally.

But the past failures and shortcomings of the American labor movement are far outweighed by the costs unionism's decline imposes on the U.S. economy, democracy, and the financial and job security of *all* workers. That is the central conclusion of The Century Foundation Task Force on the Future of Unions. The task force, which met five times over the course of eighteen months, agreed unanimously that dwindling union membership is directly related to some of the most serious problems facing the nation: gaping inequality in income and wealth, stagnating wages, inadequate pension and health insurance coverage, and growing public alienation from American politics.

It may seem boorish to highlight the shortcomings of a U.S. economy that in many respects has never been better. After all, inflation is in check, unemployment is at its lowest level in decades, economic growth is robust, borrowing costs are modest, the stock market is booming, and consumer confidence is high. Yet a little perspective is in order. Levels of income and wealth inequality, after widening to levels last experienced during the Great Depression, have narrowed only slightly despite this decade's prosperity. Median weekly wages did not return to the 1988 peak until 1998. Throughout most of that period, median incomes fell far behind the rate of improvements in labor productivity, and widespread layoffs continued despite enormous profits in many industries. From 1992 to 1995, profits rose more than 20 percent annually even as companies announced some two million layoffs. As a consequence, few workers express much confidence in the security of their jobs.

The number of Americans lacking health insurance keeps rising as the share of employers offering coverage keeps falling. And young citizens who are unable to earn a college degree—still more than half of those under the age of thirty—face rapidly declining earnings prospects compared to counterparts who complete college.

A variety of forces have roiled these perilous undercurrents beneath the glittering surface of the economy. Competition from foreign companies has forced many domestic corporations, especially in manufacturing sectors, to be far more vigilant about their costs than in the past. Former General Electric executive vice president Frank Doyle described to the task force how, in the past, his company set prices for products based on adding a reasonable profit margin to its costs; now global competition has resulted in constant pressure to reduce product prices, forcing manufacturers continually to squeeze costs—often leading to layoffs, plant relocation overseas, frugality with wages and benefits, and outsourcing of work to firms offering cheaper labor.

Heightened competition from abroad has coincided with dramatic changes in the way work is organized in many firms, relegating the once pervasive assembly line to relative obscurity. Often referred to under sobriquets such as "high-performance workplaces" or "total quality management," the newer approaches, as described by Massachusetts Institute of Technology economist Paul Osterman, have features that include (1) devolving authority and responsibility to ordinary workers (white- and blue-collar) to come up with new ideas and processes; (2) creating teams of workers who collectively try to develop the most efficient way to produce a product; (3) shifting responsibility for quality from a separate corporate unit to everyone involved in the production process; (4) viewing some workers as core to an organization while others can be managed under a different set of rules and expectations; (5) developing closer relationships with suppliers that blur lines between traditionally distinct units; and (6) introducing a variety of production process innovations like "just-in-time" inventory.

Often accompanied by extensive integration of new computer and communications technologies, these changes have required workers to develop new skills and become far more adaptable than in the past. They also have enabled firms, particularly in manufacturing, to produce a car or a ton of steel with far fewer workers than in the past.

Finally, the industrial mix of the nation's economy looks much different. The post–World War II decline in the share of workers employed in manufacturing, the long-standing stronghold of unions, continues. Among services, job categories with the highest growth rates are split between high-paying professions in health care, the law, and communications and poorly compensated jobs like child care, housecleaning, and restaurant work. Both the high- and low-end segments of the service sector have traditionally been difficult to organize for a variety of reasons. Foremost among those challenges is that relatively small numbers of workers tend to be employed in one site, leaving individuals especially vulnerable to (illegal) dismissal if they begin to talk about organizing.

In light of these fundamental transformations in the economy and the workplace, could it be possible that unions have simply outlived their purpose? After all, the Wagner National Labor Relations Act, which created the legal underpinnings for unionism, became law more than sixty years ago, in a completely different era. Might the nation be better off if organized labor simply faded into obsolescence?

The task force's answer to these questions is a resounding "No!" In the absence of powerful, organized representation, workers are extremely vulnerable on all of the fronts where corporate cost cutting has taken its toll. With the nation's economic pie growing so rapidly, workers at all income levels ought to be receiving larger paychecks, more generous pension and health care benefits, and a greater degree of job security. But instead, the trend has been in the opposite direction: from 1991 to 1997, workers' pay fell to the lowest share of national income since 1968, while the share going to profits rose to the highest level since that same year. One important reason why is that the ability of workers to communicate to their bosses effectively and with some degree of clout has eroded over time. The consequences are profound and need to be reversed.

The labor movement's decline is as unhealthy for American democracy as it is for the economic security of the nation's workers. Throughout the industrialized world, strong and vibrant unions provide information to workers about important political issues, promote voter turnout, and stimulate debate over matters of concern to average citizens that many well-heeled elites would rather ignore. Almost all nations with established, elected forms of government are characterized by a robust labor movement. Most— the United States is an exception—nurture unions in open recognition of the value they contribute to a democratic society.

In contrast to the unanimity of the task force over the need to revitalize the collective voice and strength of workers, members disagreed about the causes of the decline in unionism and about the most effective strategies for strengthening workers' influence in the future. Many members acknowledged that past union leadership was partly to blame, but to widely varying degrees. Nelson Lichtenstein's background paper to this report argues that the success of unions during their heyday engendered complacency, even arrogance, that diminished their public image and willingness to adapt to changing circumstances. But some members felt that such past mistakes had far less to do with the decline in union membership than did the broader transformations in the economy.

All members also agreed to some extent that labor laws have become outdated and excessively impede the right of workers to organize—a fundamental right in all democracies. Moreover, enforcement of the laws that exist is undermined by an overburdened National Labor Relations Board and mild sanctions that ineffectively deter transgressions. In this environment, corporations have developed a wide range of sophisticated strategies for deterring organizing efforts, campaigning against and stalling unionization votes, and, in many cases where new unions are formed, failing to reach agreement on a first contract. Some of those strategies comply with the law; many do not. In light of the weak implementation of the outmoded laws that exist, many task force members found it remarkable that any new unions have been formed at all in recent years.

Beyond that common ground, task force members held a wide range of views about what should be done to reinvigorate labor and reverse the negative consequences of its decline. Some focused on the need for unions to develop more creative and energetic organizational strategies. Others argued that no organizing effort, no matter how masterly, would be sufficient without fundamental changes in labor laws. Still other members, dubious about the political prospects for legislative changes, endorsed new ideas for organizing workers outside the model of unions. Some argued that political strategies that would appeal to the broader public also should be pursued.

The range of views on the task force about labor's future is conveyed in the comments of members appended to this statement. But for readers who are skeptical about whether the decline of unions is bad for workers and the country, the task force wants to emphasize that it uniformly believes that the case for a strong labor movement is clear-cut. Evidence abounds that unions provide enormous benefits to members and nonmembers alike.

WHAT UNIONS DO FOR MEMBERS

In the aggregate, union members earn about one-third higher wages than nonunion workers: the difference in 1996 was between $615 a week for union members and $462 a week for nonunion workers. While barely a majority of American workers are covered by employer-provided health plans, 84 percent of those in unions are. For women, Hispanics, and those whose formal education ended with high school, union membership doubles the probability of receiving health coverage; for those without a high school diploma, it triples the odds. All of these differentials remain, even after a period of corporate downsizing and layoffs in traditionally unionized industries, rounds of concession bargaining, declining strike activity, the rise of striker replacements, a shift toward merit pay and contract labor, growing reliance on foreign workers, and several years in the 1990s in which nonunion pay raises outpaced union gains.

Of course, private sector union members are more likely to be employed in manufacturing industries, which on average pay better than the service sector work that occupies about 75 percent of the workforce. But even after comparing compensation levels of union and nonunion workers in the same industries, unionized employees fare better (see Table 1).

One illustrative case is that of nursing homes, of which about 88 percent are nonunionized and 12 percent unionized. In the nonunionized facilities, the average hourly wage of a nurse's aide is about $6.06; in the unionized nursing homes, starting wages average $8 an hour. Unionized nurse's aides more frequently have health insurance, pension coverage, and other benefits like paid holidays, vacations, and a reliable schedule with guaranteed hours. They are more likely to receive tuition reimbursement that helps them to continue their education and become licensed practical nurses, a job that usually pays $12 to $14 an hour. Moreover, unionized nursing homes are more likely to have adequate supplies, more staff (and thereby more replacements when employees are ill or absent), and even better food for residents. Injuries are less common, in large part because unions have negotiated for more training and for lifting equipment.[1]

Moreover, polls of workers show that most of them recognize the benefits that a union—or some unspecified form of worker representation akin to a union—would bring to them. For example, a survey by Joel Rogers and Richard Freeman found that 82 percent of nonunion workers thought employee involvement programs geared toward improving productivity would be more effective "if employees, as a group, had more say in how these programs were run." Between 69 percent and 76 percent of nonunion workers would like to have committees that meet with management on a regular basis to discuss employment issues. And support was overwhelming for a form of representation with which management would cooperate.

In another survey conducted in 1996, Seymour Martin Lipset and Noah Meltz[2] found that 47 percent of nonunion workers polled said they would vote for a union tomorrow if an election were held, 57 percent felt that unions on the whole were good,

TABLE 1
COMPENSATION LEVELS OF UNION AND NONUNION WORKERS

	MEMBERS OF UNIONS	NON-UNION
OCCUPATION		
Managerial and professional specialty	$776	$731
Executive, administrative, and managerial	757	721
Professional specialty	782	742
Technical, sales, and administrative support	550	441
Technicians and related support	677	586
Sales occupations	467	483
Administrative support, including clerical	545	404
Service occupations	516	293
Protective service	724	418
Service, except protective service	398	283
Precision production, craft, and repair	724	501
Operators, fabricators, and laborers	572	365
Machine operators, assemblers, and inspectors	533	356
Transportation and material moving occupations	658	451
Handlers, equipment cleaners, helpers, and laborers	509	310
Farming, forestry, and fishing	505	290
INDUSTRY		
Agricultural wage and salary workers	*	305
Private nonagricultural wage and salary workers	$610	476
Mining	717	668
Construction	771	484
Manufacturing	595	503
Durable goods	619	623
Nondurable goods	536	470
Transportation and public utilities	718	580
Transportation	702	513
Communications and public utilities	746	690
Wholesale and retail trade	457	387
Wholesale trade	545	524
Retail trade	419	347
Finance, insurance, and real estate	487	548
Services	517	470
Government workers	681	530
Federal	689	678
State	628	540
Local	697	479

*Data not shown where base is less than 50,000.
Source: U.S. Bureau of Labor Statistics, "Employment and Earnings," Washington, D.C., January 1999, p. 218.

and only 37 percent felt that unions were not needed because workers were already being fairly treated.

Whether members of unions or not, the majority of American
workers also recognize the need for "voice." In today's economy, all
workers, organized or not, are expressing views about the need for a
raise, the pressure of work and family demands, and the insidiousness
of corporate greed that comport with the common union message.
According to polling by Peter D. Hart Associates and the Mellman
Group for the AFL-CIO, a majority of Americans agree that the
statement "Many families are under tremendous stress, because both
parents have to work in order to make ends meet" is a perfect
description of the current economy; they also believe it is completely accurate to say, "Nobody's job is secure today; downsizing, layoffs
and mergers can cost anyone their job, no matter how good a job
they have done for the company," and that "working hard isn't
enough anymore, because companies aren't loyal to their employees."[3] Polling and focus groups indicate that a majority of the public rate "corporate greed" as the most significant cause of the nation's
economic problems and see downsizing as a choice by management
to boost short-term profits, stock prices, and executive pay at the
expense of their employees, which makes them very angry.

> These attitudes have created something of a pendulum swing
> in . . . sympathies toward labor and management. When asked
> which side they generally favor when they hear about a dispute
> between management and workers, Americans . . . today side . . .
> with unions by a 20-point margin—up from just an eight-point
> margin at the end of 1993.[4]

Unionization significantly increases the longevity of employment
and tenure on the job, a contributor to higher earnings for union
members over time. Sixty percent of union workers have been with
their employers for at least ten years, compared to just 32.6 percent
of nonunion workers.[5] Surveys suggest that union workers have
greater job stability because they are more likely to be satisfied
with their jobs, receive better pay, have better benefits, and have
access to fair grievance procedures.

One common claim of those opposed to unions is that they
undermine productivity growth by imposing rigid work rules that

diminish management's flexibility to innovate and adapt quickly to changing markets. But most research to date suggests that labor productivity is actually higher in unionized than nonunionized firms in the same industry.[6] The work of Freeman and others has demonstrated that unions can increase productivity by reducing turnover, strengthening the influence of workers in decisionmaking about the production process, and generally providing cooperative labor-management relations, including in the areas of quality assurance and training programs, at the plant level.[7] Indeed, the decline in U.S. labor productivity from 1973 to 1998 would be difficult to pin on unions in light of their shrinking membership over that period. Table 2 summarizes assessments from different research studies about the effect of unions on productivity in various industries.

TABLE 2
UNIONS AND PRODUCTIVITY

INDUSTRY	UNION PRODUCTIVITY EFFECT (%)	YEAR OF STUDY
Manufacturing	19–24	1978
Construction	17–38	1984 & 1987
Cement Plants	6–12	1980
Hospitals	0–16	1984 & 1988
Banking	0	1985
Furniture	15	1976

Source: Dale Belman, "Unions, the Quality of Labor Relations, and Firm Performance," in Lawrence Mishel and Paul B. Voos, Unions and Economic Competitiveness (Armonk, N.Y.: M.E. Sharpe, Inc., 1992), pp. 41–107.

Recent academic work also shows that unionized firms are no more or less likely than nonunionized firms either to thrive, go out of business, move plants overseas, or lay off large numbers of workers.[8] In instances when employers have faced serious financial pressure, unions have often participated in remedial efforts such as wage and benefit concessions in collective bargaining, the introduction of new technology, an infusion of workers' capital, or sharing ownership to restore a firm's competitiveness.

Yet, there is more to what unions do than improving wages and benefits and increasing productivity. They provide a "voice" for workers—the ability to participate in the democratic process, through collective bargaining and other means.[9] Unions are the conduit for workers to communicate with both employers and political leaders. Having collective representation in the workplace overcomes the "free rider" problem endemic in actions whose benefits are indivisible, as well as the very real threat of retaliation to an individual speaking up alone. Over the years, unions have been the driving force behind legislation raising the minimum wage, expanding Medicare coverage, strengthening pension insurance, bolstering federal job training and placement programs, and providing family and medical leave—changes that benefit all workers. Unions can provide workplace justice more effectively and cheaply than the courts in many respects, particularly in matters such as race and gender discrimination.

WHAT UNIONS DO FOR ALL AMERICANS

The erosion of organized representation in the workplace is imposing severe costs on all Americans. Academic research based on data from the 1970s, when unions were substantially stronger than they are now, indicated that the wages of employees in large, nonunion firms were raised by between 10 percent and 20 percent because of unions. That so-called spillover effect was largely attributable to employers wanting to deter the formation of unions on their own premises or simply to keep their compensation levels in the same ballpark with unionized companies.[10] Similarly, evidence is abundant that unions were almost exclusively responsible for inducing companies to offer generous pensions and health insurance, a practice that spread to many nonunion companies.

Of course, it is difficult to prove with certainty that declining unionism in and of itself caused overlapping trends like wage stagnation, rising income inequality, reduced employee benefits, and a fraying in the underpinnings of American democracy. For one thing, most of those problems only reared their heads in the early 1970s or later—long after the decline in union power was well under way. Moreover, so many forces could conceivably have contributed to the difficulties cited that isolating unionization is technically almost impossible.

But taking such caveats into account, the task force believes that declining unionization unquestionably played a significant role in those undesirable developments. Since the mission of unions is to resist encroachments on the well-being of workers, and since unions in the past have demonstrated their effectiveness in protecting their gains, we feel confident that the decline of unions has had something to do with those trends. Here is why.

Wage Stagnation

The wage of the median worker in the United States, after adjusting for inflation, soared during the 1960s, remained roughly the same in the 1970s, and then actually dropped in the 1980s and the first half of the 1990s. Because the unionized share of the workforce fell steadily throughout the entire period, the connection between unionization and wage levels at first glance would not seem to be apparent (see Figure 1, page 14). But economist Thomas Palley of the AFL-CIO, in a recent unpublished paper, develops an uncannily strong connection between union "density" (extent of union penetration as a proportion of the labor force) and the share of economic output going to labor (total hourly compensation divided by output per hour) (see Figure 2, page 14). Without delving into the technical analysis involved, Palley shows that the connections between the decline in union density and the shrinkage in the share of the economic pie going to labor are not coincidental.

Intuitively, it would be difficult to argue that there is little or no connection between wage levels and the extent of unionization. The primary goal of most unions in most settings is to elevate wages, and the evidence presented earlier amply shows that unionized workplaces pay more than nonunionized counterparts. In the past, those gains spilled over into the nonunionized sector. But, as the threat of unionization has weakened over time, those spillover effects appear to have diminished.

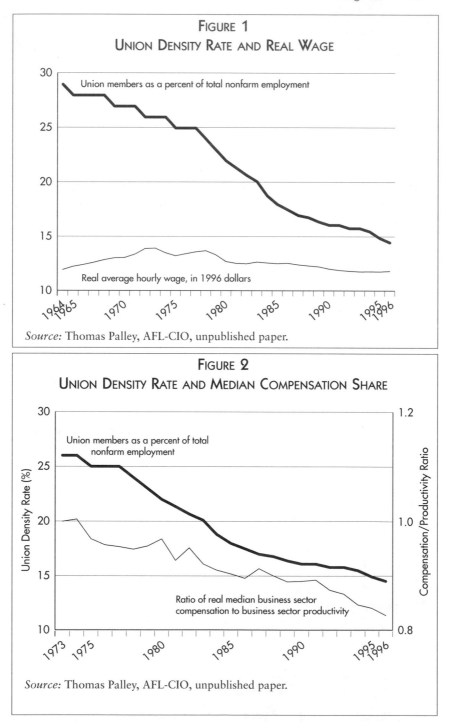

FIGURE 1
UNION DENSITY RATE AND REAL WAGE

Union members as a percent of total nonfarm employment

Real average hourly wage, in 1996 dollars

Source: Thomas Palley, AFL-CIO, unpublished paper.

FIGURE 2
UNION DENSITY RATE AND MEDIAN COMPENSATION SHARE

Union members as a percent of total nonfarm employment

Union Density Rate (%)

Compensation/Productivity Ratio

Ratio of real median business sector compensation to business sector productivity

Source: Thomas Palley, AFL-CIO, unpublished paper.

Income Inequality

A wide range of studies have demonstrated that gaps in income and wealth between the rich and poor have widened dramatically over the past twenty-five years, diminishing only slightly of late thanks mainly to very low unemployment rates. As with wage stagnation, the trend toward greater inequality has been blamed on increased globalization, technological changes, the decline of the manufacturing sector, the booming stock market, and changes in government fiscal and monetary policy. Although those processes certainly contributed to rising inequality to some extent, the task force is convinced that the decline of unions also has played an important role in deepening the chasm between rich and poor.

Traditionally, unions have negotiated wage packages that narrow earnings differentials and have tended to improve wages most for workers with modest educational backgrounds—the same people who have experienced the greatest decline in earnings prospects over the past twenty-five years. It is largely because unions are more prevalent in manufacturing industries that wage ranges are commonly bound tighter in manufacturing than in most services.

Studies by economists Richard Freeman of Harvard and David Card of Princeton reinforce the impact of deunionization on inequality levels. Table 3 (see page 16) breaks down the decline in unionization from 1978 to 1988 for different categories of workers, as well as the union wage premium—the amount unionized workers are paid above comparable nonunion workers—for the same categories. What the table shows is that, in large part because union representation fell dramatically among blue-collar and high school–educated workers, who enjoyed high union wage premiums, gaps widened between white- and blue-collar workers and between those who had a college education and those who had attended only high school.[11]

In Table 4 (see page 17), Card shows the impact of deunionization on workers at different income levels. Unionization declined among workers in the lowest fifth of the income distribution from 1973 to 1987 by 15.4 percent, while it actually increased by 7.2 percent for the top fifth. Because union members in the bottom fifth enjoyed a 27.9 percent higher wage than nonunion counterparts,

TABLE 3
EFFECT OF DEUNIONIZATION ON MALE OCCUPATION AND EDUCATION DIFFERENTIALS, 1978–88 (IN PERCENT)

A. EFFECTS OF UNION DECLINE ON WAGES*

GROUP	UNION WAGE PREMIUM**	PERCENTAGE IN UNIONS		CHANGE, 1978–88	EFFECT OF UNION DECLINE ON WAGES
		1978	1988		
By Occupation					
White-collar	1	18	13	-5	-0.1
Blue-collar	26	47	33	-14	-3.6
Difference					3.5
By Education					
College	-2	17	14	-3	0.1
High School	16	42	30	-12	-1.4
Difference					1.5

B. CONTRIBUTION OF DEUNIONIZATION TO HIGHER WAGE DIFFERENTIALS*

	CHANGE IN WAGE DIFFERENTIAL, 1978–88*	UNION DECLINE EFFECT ON WAGE DIFFERENTIAL	HIGHER DIFFERENTIAL EXPLAINED BY UNION DECLINE
White-collar/Blue-collar	7	3.5	50
College/High School	6	1.5	25

* Differentials and change in differentials computed in natural log percentage points.
** Controlling for workforce characteristics.

Source: Richard B. Freeman, "How Much Has De-Unionization Contributed to the Rise in Male Earnings Inequality?" working paper no. 3826, National Bureau of Economic Research, Cambridge, Mass., 1991.

TABLE 4

EFFECT OF UNIONS ON WAGES, BY QUINTILE, 1973–87

	LOWEST FIFTH	SECOND FIFTH	MIDDLE FIFTH	FOURTH FIFTH	TOP FIFTH	AVERAGE
Percentage of Workers in Unions						
1973	39.9	43.7	38.3	33.5	12.5	33.7
1987	23.5	30.3	33.1	24.7	17.7	26.4
Change, 1973–87	-15.4	-13.4	-5.2	-8.8	7.2	-7.3
Wage Effect of Union (in percent)						
Union Wage, 1987	27.9	16.2	18.0	0.9	10.5	15.9
Average Wage, 1987	6.6	4.9	6.0	2.1	2.1	4.2
Wage Effect of Deunionization						
1973–87	-4.3	-2.2	-0.9	-0.1	0.8	-1.1

Source: David Card, "The Effect of Unions on the Distribution of Wages: Redistribution or Relabelling?" working paper no. 287, Department of Economics, Princeton University, 1991.

the decline in membership for that quintile implies a 4.3 percent reduction in average wages below what they would otherwise be. In contrast, the top fifth actually earned 0.8 percent more on average because of the increase in union membership it experienced.[12]

In another analysis, the AFL-CIO's Thomas Palley shows that median compensation—the pay level for an individual relative to whom half of the workforce earns more and half less—has fallen behind the rate of productivity growth since 1973. Over the same period, average compensation—which gives greater weight to the earnings of high-income workers—has kept pace with productivity improvements (see Figure 3, page 18). In the past, median wages also grew at roughly the same rate as productivity increases. The logical deduction is that a greater share of the overall wage pie is going to higher-income workers. At the same time, as Figure 4 (see page 18) shows, the ratio of median to average compensation has declined at roughly the same pace as union density. Those correlations imply a connection between declining unionization and rising inequality, although they do not prove one.

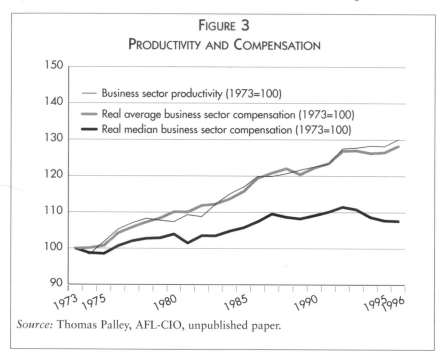

FIGURE 3
PRODUCTIVITY AND COMPENSATION

Source: Thomas Palley, AFL-CIO, unpublished paper.

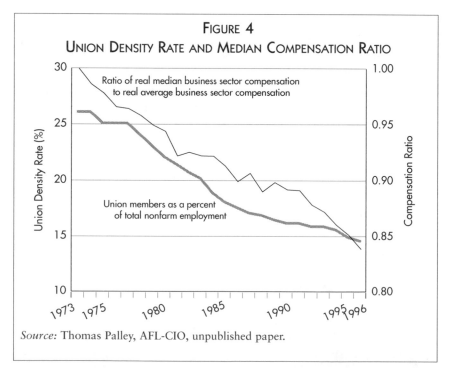

FIGURE 4
UNION DENSITY RATE AND MEDIAN COMPENSATION RATIO

Source: Thomas Palley, AFL-CIO, unpublished paper.

The growing gaps between the rich and poor mean that the benefits of economic prosperity are increasingly flowing to the upper crust while Americans facing the greatest financial pressures are experiencing little or no relief. The task force emphatically believes that this trend is harmful not only to the poor but also to U.S. society as a whole. Everyone will bear enormous costs if the nation continues to tolerate childhood poverty rates of nearly 25 percent, underfinanced and ineffective schools, and workers with insufficient training to earn a decent living.

Shrinking Employee Benefits

Since 1979, the proportion of all U.S. workers whose employers provide pensions and health insurance has declined. For both pensions and health insurance, coverage rates arc lowest and have declined the most for the least-educated workers—those whom labor unions have traditionally represented.

The story on pensions is summarized in Table 5 (see page 20), which shows that the fraction of private sector workers who were covered by pensions declined from 48 percent to 45 percent between 1979 and 1993.[13] Among workers without a high school diploma, pension coverage plummeted from 41 percent to 25 percent. At the same time, the nature of pensions available to those who receive some kind of coverage has been transformed.[14] In the past, most pensions were defined-benefit plans that paid retirement checks based entirely on the level of wages that workers received during their careers. Defined-benefit pensions have increasingly been replaced by defined-contribution plans like 401(k)s, in which benefits depend on how much workers choose to contribute to the plan (often with a matching payment from the employer) and on how much the investments in the account increase (or decrease) in value. The shift from defined-benefit to defined-contribution plans has, in effect, pushed the risks and responsibility for providing adequate retirement coverage from employers to employees.

Table 6 (see page 21) tells the story for employer-provided health care coverage.[15] Among all workers, health insurance coverage declined from 71 percent in 1979 to 64 percent in 1993. Those without a high school diploma experienced a drop in coverage

TABLE 5
CHANGE IN PRIVATE SECTOR EMPLOYER-PROVIDED PENSION COVERAGE, 1979–93

Group*	Pension Coverage (%)			
	1979	1988	1993	Change, 1979–93
ALL WORKERS	48	44	45	-3
GENDER				
Men	55	48	47	-8
Women	37	39	42	5
RACE/ETHNICITY				
White	50	47	47	-3
Black	45	39	42	-3
Hispanic	35	28	29	-6
EDUCATION				
Less than High School	41	31	25	-16
High School	49	44	44	-5
Some College	49	44	46	-3
College	56	54	55	-1
More than College	60	58	59	-1
WAGE QUINTILE				
Lowest	18	14	13	-5
Second	35	33	34	-1
Middle	51	45	51	0
Fourth	68	59	61	-7
Top	76	69	72	-4

* Private sector wage and salary workers, age 18–24, with at least 20 weekly hours and 26 weeks of work.

Source: Lawrence Mishel, Jared Bernstein, and John Schmitt, *The State of Working America 1996–97*, Economic Policy Institute Series (Armonk, N.Y.: M. E. Sharpe, Inc., 1997), p. 160.

from 63 percent to 45 percent. Although the total amount of money (adjusted for inflation) that corporations spent on health insurance and other benefits increased over the period, largely because of rapidly rising medical costs, a declining share of the workforce receives a full package of employer-provided benefits.

Once again, a variety of forces have undoubtedly contributed to these trends. But the declining membership and clout of labor unions has unquestionably weakened pressure on companies—

TABLE 6
CHANGE IN PRIVATE SECTOR EMPLOYER-PROVIDED
HEALTH INSURANCE COVERAGE, 1979–93

Group*	Health Insurance Coverage (%)			
	1979	1988	1993	Change, 1979–93
ALL WORKERS	71	69	64	-7
GENDER				
Men	76	74	68	-8
Women	61	62	58	-5
RACE/ETHNICITY				
White	72	71	66	-6
Black	66	64	61	-5
Hispanic	63	56	47	-16
EDUCATION				
Less than High School	63	55	45	-18
High School	70	67	62	-8
Some College	72	68	63	-9
College	81	82	75	-6
More than College	80	85	79	-1
WAGE QUINTILE				
Lowest	40	32	27	-8
Second	66	62	59	-7
Middle	79	76	71	-6
Fourth	87	83	80	-7
Top	90	90	87	-3

* Private sector wage and salary workers, age 18–64, with at least 20 weekly hours and 26 weeks of work.

Source: Lawrence Mishel, Jared Bernstein, and John Schmitt, *The State of Working America 1996–97*, Economic Policy Institute Series (Armonk, N.Y.: M.E. Sharpe, Inc., 1997), p. 159.

both unionized and nonunionized—to maintain generous benefit packages. The creation and expansion of employee benefit packages in previous decades was largely a consequence of the collective bargaining process, as Nelson Lichtenstein's paper describes. Richard Freeman and James Medoff have demonstrated that nonunionized companies felt compelled to offer comparable benefits of their own. Now that those pressures have abated, it is no coincidence that a smaller share of the workforce receives decent pension and health insurance coverage. And the steep decline in coverage among less-educated workers provides an especially strong indication that the shrinkage of unions is responsible to a significant extent.

Worrisome Changes in American Democracy

The decline in voter turnout in recent decades is well documented. Underlying that clear-cut trend has been an apparent weakening in what Harvard political scientist Robert Putnam calls "civic engagement."[16] Putnam highlights the decline in membership since the early 1960s not only in labor unions but in virtually every organized social activity outside of work in the United States—from the PTA to the Knights of Columbus to most religions to Boy Scouts to bowling leagues. Alluding to Alexis de Tocqueville's insights about the importance of such private associations to democracy in pre–Civil War America, Putnam raises concerns that declining participation in such functions may be weakening the nation's social fabric. Institutions like labor unions, Kiwanis clubs, and even bowling leagues encourage individuals to communicate with others about shared concerns. Those interactions often prompt people to take an interest in problems facing their community, engaging them in activities like volunteering, charitable giving, and voting. Individuals who do not participate in such organized activities, Putnam argues, are less likely to care enough about issues facing their community to do so much as vote.

Although the causes of declining participation in labor unions and the other institutions Putnam highlights are manifold and complex, the task force agrees that American democracy is worse off as a result. Labor unions have been the single most important agent for social justice in the United States. They have played a vital role in originating a national debate over the sharing of the riches of economic growth, and they have been a leading force in opening up opportunity to all working people. For those without economic power—the unorganized and lowest paid—increases in the minimum wage and a safety net of social programs were delivered on the political battlefield and paid for by a growing economy.

The public, when polled, expresses support for the products of unionization: job security, health benefits, better pay, and pensions for retirement. But they are by and large unfavorably disposed toward unions themselves. This negative image and reputation presents perhaps the most formidable obstacle facing the American labor movement. The task force finds it critical that the labor movement again be seen to represent, in the broadest possible terms, the concerns and interests of all Americans.

Unions are very American institutions, elemental to our democracy and our society. Unions are institutions where workers exercise their right of association and of expression. Unions are institutions that integrate women and men of all ethnic, religious, and skill groups. Unions are institutions in which working people exercise leadership, solve problems, negotiate, and learn political skills. In short, unions are democratic institutions, with the natural flaws inherent to democracy. They are neither expendable nor disposable. Unions are good for democracy, not only in places such as Poland but also here, in the United States of America.

NOTES

1. From Paul Osterman, *Securing Prosperity* (Princeton, N.J.: Princeton University Press, 1999), a Century Foundation Book, pp. 169–70.

2. Seymour Martin Lipset and Noah Meltz, "Work and Institutions," *Perspectives on Work* 1, no. 3 (December 1997): 18.

3. "The Economic Situation Facing Working Families: Americans' Attitudes toward the Economy, Living Standards, and Corporate Behavior," mimeo, Washington, D.C., Peter D. Hart Associates and the Mellman Group, 1996.

4. Ibid., p. 18.

5. AFL-CIO analysis of the *Current Population Survey, Supplement on Employee Benefits,* Washington, D.C., April 1993.

6. Richard Freeman and James L. Medoff, "Trade Unions and Productivity: Some New Evidence on an Old Issue," working Paper no. 1249, National Bureau of Economic Research, Cambridge, Mass., 1983, p. 10.

7. Richard B. Freeman and James L. Medoff, *What Do Unions Do?* (New York: Basic Books, 1984).

8. This conclusion is from David C. Johnston, "On Payday, Union Jobs Stack Up Very Well," *New York Times*, August 31, 1997.

9. See A. O. Hirschman, *Exit, Voice, and Loyalty: Responses to Decline in Firms, Organizations, and States* (Cambridge, Mass.: Harvard University Press, 1970) and Freeman and Medoff, *What Do Unions Do?*

10. Freeman and Medoff, *What Do Unions Do?*

11. Richard B. Freeman, "How Much Has De-Unionization Contributed to the Rise in Male Earnings Inequality?" working paper no. 3826, National Bureau of Economic Research, Cambridge, Mass., 1991.

12. David Card, "The Effect of Unions on the Distribution of Wages: Redistribution or Relabelling?" working paper no. 287, Department of Economics, Princeton University, 1991.

13. Lawrence Mishel, Jared Bernstein, and John Schmitt, *The State of Working America 1996–97,* Economic Policy Institute Series (Armonk, N.Y.: M. E. Sharpe, Inc., 1997), p. 160.

14. Ibid., p. 161.

15. Ibid., p. 159.

16. Robert Putnam, "Bowling Alone: America's Declining Social Capital," *Journal of Democracy* 6, no. 1 (January 1995): 65–78.

STATEMENTS OF
TASK FORCE MEMBERS

STATEMENT OF JAY MAZUR, DAVID SMITH, AND ROBERT WELSH

As this report makes clear, the American labor movement must respond on many levels to the great challenge it faces. There is no question that change must come first from within, a process that is well under way. The commitment to and new resources for organizing have begun to yield results, as has the mobilization of our base in the political arena. New international programs are being developed on the basis of strategic industrial objectives. Corporate campaigns are increasingly sophisticated, a multifaceted mix of workplace actions, coalition politics, financial leverage, and public relations that can and often does reach the global scope of the employer. There is, of course, much more to be done, new ideas to be tested and old traditions to be renewed in the crucible of struggle, if the labor movement is to fulfill its historic mission of extending the blessings of democracy to the masses of working people.

This will not happen, however, without changing our archaic labor laws. There is little to be gained here by engaging in chicken-and-egg arguments about whether these laws are the cause or result of a weakened labor movement. They are both. The relationship between movement and laws is symbiotic, with weakness feeding off weakness in a downward spiral. The downspin must be reversed, but this cannot be done without addressing, directly and in detail, the law.

One of the great strengths of American democracy is its insistence on the rule of law. Whenever laws have failed to reflect our values as a society or failed to regulate behavior in accord with those values, the consequences have been disastrous. Reforming our labor laws is not a magic bullet. Further, acquiring the political authority to change them will require strengthening the movement in many of the ways discussed in this report. It would be a fatal mistake, however, to ignore the profound impact that our labor laws have had on the erosion of union strength over the past forty years.

In this context, we would point out that a 1935 report of the Twentieth Century Fund played a critical role in the public and legislative debates that led to the passage of the National Labor

Relations Act (NLRA). While the current report describes the decline in union representation and its adverse consequences, it does not adequately link these problems to the degeneration of U.S. labor laws or point toward new legislative solutions.

Federal labor law guarantees private sector workers "the right to self-organization, to form, join or assist labor organizations" and "to bargain collectively through representatives of their own choosing." Under current law, however, these rights are illusory.

Both of the fundamental processes of worker representation—union organizing and collective bargaining—are fundamentally flawed within the current statutory framework. The procedures for obtaining union recognition are not only inconsistent with basic principles of democratic government, they also allow employers to thwart workers' desire to be represented by a union. Furthermore, even if workers overcome these obstacles and a union is certified as their representative for purposes of collective bargaining, they often find that the employer's legal duty to bargain in good faith with the union is not only without substance but easily evaded. In many cases the union and employer never reach an agreement.

Under the current law, government-supervised elections are the only mechanism through which workers can oblige their employer to recognize their chosen representative. Yet, the election process has three fundamental flaws.

First, the electoral process allows employers to exert significant influence on voters despite the facts that elections decide only whether workers will be represented in their dealings with the employer and employers, quite properly, cannot cast ballots and are not candidates. Nevertheless, the procedures used in representation elections allow employers to influence the timing of the election and the composition of the voting unit as well as to campaign for a no vote.

Employers exert substantial influence on elections, in part because union elections are conducted only after employees file a petition seeking an election and the National Labor Relations Board (NLRB) decides that the requested voting unit is an appropriate one. Since the Taft-Hartley Act amended the NLRA in 1947, federal law has required that a hearing take place subsequent to the filing of a petition and before the election. The Board has defined employers as parties to these pre-election hearings, thereby enabling them to influence the composition of the unit. By choosing to litigate every possible issue, employers can also use the hearing to postpone elections for many months or to pressure unions to accede to a disadvantageous election date or definition of voting unit in order to avoid delay.

Second, employers have overwhelming advantages over unions in campaigns. The Board has held that it is ordinarily lawful for employers to campaign in the workplace—the only place where all voters gather—while barring union organizers from the premises. The unequal access to voters persists up through election day itself, for NLRB procedures provide that elections should ordinarily be held at the workplace. Thus, employers can continue campaigning until workers enter the polls to cast their ballot, but union organizers cannot.

Employers' advantages in campaigns are based not only on their control of the workplace but also on their control of workers. While unions must obtain signatures from 30 percent of the workers in a unit simply to initiate the representation process, unions often cannot discover who the workers are or locate them, for increasingly workers do not work at a common worksite. Under the current law, an employer need not provide the union with a list of its workers until seven days after the posthearing decision directing that an election be held—ordinarily only three weeks before the election. Thus, in many instances, unions must campaign up to the very eve of the election without even knowing who the voters are or where to find them.

But employers' control over the voters in representation elections is still more profound. Employers have the legal right to direct workers to sit and listen to a campaign speech intended to persuade them to vote against representation. In other words, employees can be fired for refusing to listen to their employer's antiunion speech and instead returning to work. With respect to such "captive audience" meetings, the Board has held that workers have "no statutorily protected right to leave a meeting which the employees were required by management to attend . . . to listen to management's noncoercive antiunion speech." An employee can even be fired for persisting in an attempt to ask questions or express a contrary view after an employer has informed the captive audience of workers that there will be no questions.

The outcome of the unequal access to and control over voters in union elections is clear: employers convey their message while unions do not. In one of the most comprehensive empirical studies of union election campaigns to date, Julius Getman of the University of Texas and Stephen Goldberg of Northwestern University found that while 83 percent of employees attended at least one employer-sponsored meeting, only 36 percent attended a union meeting. More important, employers are able to reach undecided voters, while unions usually reach only the converted.

Finally, employers' advantages stem from the economic power they exercise over workers. Employers can lawfully fire the vast majority of unrepresented workers at will—for no reason at all. This power stands behind every statement of opinion voiced by employers concerning union elections. As early as 1940 the NLRB informed Congress that behind what an employer says "lies the full weight of his economic position, based upon his control over the livelihood of his employees." The same year the Supreme Court noted that "slight suggestions" of employer preference have a "telling effect among men who know the consequences of incurring that employer's strong displeasure." Although, in the Board's words, employer speech has "a force stronger than . . . that of persuasion," since 1947 federal law has guaranteed employers' right to speak freely in representation election campaigns.

The "free speech proviso" does not allow threats or acts of retaliation; nonetheless, employers often violate the law. Federal law bars firing workers for supporting a union. Still, according to Paul Weiler of Harvard University, one out of every twenty union supporters is fired during the course of an election campaign. Though Weiler's statistics have been questioned, even his harshest critics, Professors Bernard Meltzer and Robert LaLonde of the University of Chicago, find that employers unlawfully fire union supporters during 20 percent of all campaigns. Employers are encouraged to violate the law by the inadequate remedies available to workers and unions under existing statute. By firing key union supporters, employers often break an organizing drive. However, even if the fired employees succeed, after prolonged litigation, in proving that their employer was motivated by antiunion animus, they will collect merely back pay minus any interim earnings. In 1980 the average back pay awarded in discriminatory discharge cases was $2,000, and employers could delay entry into force of an enforceable order to pay for an average of more than four years from the filing of a complaint simply by exhausting the appeal process. Employers pay nothing for the damage their actions cause either to other employees whose exercise of their right to support a union is chilled by an illegal firing or to unions whose organizing drives are unlawfully thwarted.

The third major flaw in the electoral process is the lack of finality. After a union election either the union or the employer can file objections to the conduct of the vote. The results of the election are not certified until the Board rules on these objections, often after an evidentiary hearing. Furthermore, if an employer is not satisfied with the Board's ruling, it is effectively entitled to appeal. Employers accomplish this simply by refusing to bargain with the union even after the Board rejects the employer's objections and certifies the union as the employees' representative. When the Board cites the employer for refusing to bargain, the employer can seek review in a court of appeals. Only after a ruling in the court of appeals—usually years after the election—does the employer have a legally enforceable obligation to bargain. Moreover, there is no parallel device through which unions can obtain review of adverse Board decisions in the courts.

Upon affirmation of a Board order to bargain in a court of appeals, workers have an enforceable right to engage in collective bargaining with their employer. Yet the process of collective bargaining also has three fundamental flaws.

First, the law specifies that employers are bound neither to reach agreement with unions nor even to make any concession in collective bargaining. The employer's obligation is simply a formal one—to appear at the bargaining table and exchange proposals. If, upon bargaining, the parties reach no agreement, the employer is entitled unilaterally to change terms and conditions of employment.

Even the formal legal duty to bargain in good faith carries little force. For failing to bargain employers may be charged with committing an unfair labor practice. But the sole remedy for such a violation of federal law is an order that the employer desist from the unlawful behavior. The Board cannot impose an agreement, nor is a monetary remedy available either to punish the employer or to compensate employees denied better wages, benefits, or working conditions by the employer's unlawful actions.

Second, the law has been construed in a manner that deprives workers of the economic power that was to have been the motor of the collective bargaining process. The right to strike is protected against employer interference, restraint, and coercion by the literal terms of federal law, but the protections enacted by Congress were undercut almost as soon as they were signed into law by the Supreme Court's 1938 ruling in *NLRB* v. *Mackay Radio & Telegraph Co.* that employers can permanently replace striking workers. Employees who exercise their right to strike thus risk losing their jobs to permanent replacements while retaining only a right to be recalled should positions open. This prospect has made it nearly impossible for most workers to mount a credible strike threat in order to convince their employer to come to terms on a collective bargaining agreement.

Third, workers employed by one employer are restricted in their ability to issue peaceful appeals either to other workers or to the public for support in contract negotiations. These restrictions on "secondary activity" make it unlawful for workers seeking a contract with one employer to ask employees of another firm doing business with theirs to strike in support of their efforts. It is also unlawful for workers to carry picket signs on public sidewalks surrounding a firm that does business with their employer even if the picketing is peaceful and does not block access and if the picket signs merely request that consumers not patronize the firm. Workers are thus denied a form of protest available to all other citizens.

For engaging in such peaceful, communicative activity, unions face sanctions more severe and more swiftly delivered than those faced by employers who commit unfair labor practices. While workers can seek relief only from the slow-moving NLRB, employers alleging injury owing to unlawful "secondary" pressure can file both a charge with the Board and a lawsuit in federal court. Moreover, the Board is required by law to give priority to such employer charges, and, if it finds probable cause to believe they have merit, the Board is required to seek preliminary injunctive relief against the union in court. If an employer unlawfully fires union supporters, no such requirement is imposed on the Board.

Because of these flaws in the system of collective bargaining, workers' elected representatives are often unable to secure an agreement with employers. One study found that one-third of newly elected unions were unable to obtain a first contract; another one-quarter failed to obtain a successor agreement. Five years after they had voted for union representation, more than one-half of all such workers were not covered by collective bargaining agreements, and one-half of all workers were denied the right to bargain collectively that is theoretically protected by the law.

This is the reality that workers face daily in the struggle for their democratic rights in the workplace. Laws originally designed to protect those rights are now routinely and systematically used to subvert them. These laws will not be changed overnight, but the movement to strengthen the voice of labor in our democratic discourse must recognize the obstacle they represent to a more just and decent society.

Statement of Lewis B. Kaden, Eugene Keilin, Carol O'Cleireacain, and Bruce Simon

The report says a lot—but it leaves a great deal more to be said.

First, we emphasize our agreement with the report's basic message: the decline of unionism is bad for America. It is bad for our economy. It is bad for our democracy. It has harmed the financial and job security of all workers, not just unionized workers. In short, "the task force wants to emphasize that it uniformly believes that the case for a strong labor movement is clear-cut" (page 7).

We also applaud the report's effective debunking of some of the common myths invoked to discredit unions. The report notes that research indicates "that labor productivity is actually higher in unionized than nonunionized firms in the same industry" (page 11) and that "unionized firms are no more or less likely than nonunionized firms either to thrive, go out of business, move plants overseas, or lay off large numbers of workers" (page 11). It also highlights the role that unions have played in building a fairer and more just America, noting that "labor unions have been the single most important agent for social justice in the United States" (page 22) and that "unions are very American institutions, elemental to our democracy and our society. . . . Unions are good for democracy, not only in places such as Poland but also here, in the United States of America" (page 23).

So far so good. But where is the rest? If unions are essential to our national well-being, why do they represent only 14 percent of the nation's workforce (and only 10 percent of the nongovernmental workforce)? Why has that percentage of the workforce dropped by more than 50 percent in thirty-five years? And what should be done—and by whom—to increase union density and therefore improve the commonweal?

The report reflects disagreements among the members of the task force as to the causes of the decline in unionization and the most effective strategies for strengthening workers in the future. There was general agreement that the nation's labor laws were no longer effective, that corporations engage in strategies (some lawful, many not) to thwart unionization, that past union leadership was partly to blame, that transformations in the economy (for example, moving from the traditional, manufacturing, blue-collar base to a services-oriented and now information-driven one; also taking heed of the emergence of the "virtual" workplace and the growing dependence on a large "contingent" work force) made successful union organizing difficult. All of that reflects the common wisdom.

Different task force members ascribed varying degrees of primacy to those forces. And, to some extent, where one comes out on the primary causes shapes one's view of the strategies to restore union influence. For example, if one concludes that there is a virulent, antiunion corporate mind-set that often prompts an aggressive campaign to fire employees engaged in organizing activity, and that the current laws are inadequate to stop it, then one is moved to emphasize the need for labor law reform. A similar analysis of the other identified "causes" for the decline of unionization would produce different sets of strategies.

But we believe that the blame assessment exercise is ultimately unproductive and has proved to be a diversion. For example, even if all were to agree with the "virulent, antiunion corporate mind-set" diagnosis, there is no reason to expect that the current, or a foreseeable, Congress would pass a sufficiently rigorous series of amendments to the nation's labor laws to make a significant difference.

Instead, *we place our focus here on setting out what the labor movement can do with its own resources to help itself.*

What Must Unions Do?

If there is to be a real future for American unions, they have to change. Much of the labor movement now recognizes this. For the first time since its creation, the AFL-CIO has a leader who had to challenge the incumbent in order to take the helm, an action that has given rise to renewed interest in and much speculation about labor's direction. In addition, the new leadership has set itself the goal of revitalizing the labor movement. It will not be easy. Unions, as membership-based institutions, may still lack the incentive and sense of urgency necessary for fundamental change.

Like many other American institutions at the end of the twentieth century, unions have to craft their own future and remake themselves. In doing so, they must face up to the ways in which their failure to adapt magnifies the forces contributing to their dwindling membership and strength. First, the orientation of labor unions is defensive, holding onto and consolidating pockets of strength. In protecting those pockets, they act, look, and sound increasingly like a narrow special-interest group, a characterization that opponents seize on. This is reinforced by the various ways in which the economy is growing away from them. Second, as the face and shape of the labor force has changed, the labor movement has not. A younger, female, and minority workforce sees a labor movement speaking and acting for, as well as looking like, an older, male, and white membership. So, at the same time as its membership shrinks, its concerns are less relevant to workers in the growing sectors of the economy.

Much of the public, with no direct experience of unions, has at best no well-formed attitude toward them; at worst, there is an overtly hostile attitude that "they cannot help me." The public, when polled, expresses support for the products of unionization: job security, health benefits, better pay, and pensions for retirement. But they are surprisingly negative toward unions themselves. There is a real disconnection between what workers want and the word "union." This negative image and reputation presents, perhaps, the most formidable obstacle that must be overcome. Clearly, something is wrong in the way that unions govern and present themselves.

We think it is critically important that the labor movement again be seen to represent, in the broadest possible terms, the concerns and interests of all American workers. We note that the Service Employees International Union, led by John Sweeney, recognized that it had to speak about the issues that mattered to the workers in the new economy, and by doing so it grew. Now the union movement has chosen him to lead the AFL-CIO, and as his first political act he led the fight to raise the federal minimum wage, an issue of most benefit to workers without unions.

Taking the cue from the new leadership at the top of the premier American labor federation, we call on America's unions to organize and adapt themselves to the changed economy and workforce and recommend that the American labor movement:

1. Organize and focus strength in strategic sectors of the economy.

Absent all else, unions must stem the erosion of their numbers. In this decade alone, union membership has declined from 16.7 million (1990) to 16.1 million (1997). With the changing structure of employment and labor force growth, unions need to add each year about 128,000 new members to keep the rolls from falling and about 300,000 new members to keep the same density (14 percent of total employment and 10 percent of employment in the private sector). This is the *minimum* goal; as yet, it is not being met.

To reach President Sweeney's goal of representing 30 percent of the workforce would require American unions to recruit about twenty-five million more workers—one million a year for a quarter of a century or five million a year for the next five years. With organizing costs running at $1,000 per new member, to add one million each year would require $1 billion, about 20 percent of labor's annual income. The magnitude of such a task, and the relentlessness needed to complete it, would be unprecedented for American unions in the postwar era.

To stave off further losses and to begin to grow again requires a huge push toward organizing, including a number of different approaches to the task.

- ◆ *Seeking targets of opportunity.* With the need for numbers and victories quickly, as well as momentum, there is a strong case to be made for following the path of least resistance. This approach is about running harder to stay in place—organizing, first, enough bodies to prevent the erosion of union density and then incrementally more workers to begin the long slog back toward historically higher representation rates. This means adding those that are the easiest to organize, such as more public employees, college support workers, health technicians and professionals, and service workers, but doing so through much expanded efforts. Many of these new members will be low paid, and many will be women and minorities.

- ◆ *Controlling the commanding heights.* As difficult as it may be, the labor movement must counter the erosion in traditional, highly paid sectors, such as autos and steel.

Fundamentally, this is not a numbers issue. These industries are not where employment is growing in the new economy. But the nonunion employers offer a direct challenge to unionized employers and, ultimately, competition for market share in industries where the economies of scale in production determine costs, profit, and long-term viability. In steel, nonunion minimills, which began as niche manufacturers, are now the leaders in pricing in two of five product lines and pose an increasingly credible threat that the large, unionized steel operations will eventually be the ones forced into operating in niches where they will be able to charge the higher prices needed to cover their lost economies of scale. In automobiles, a number of foreign producers, unionized in their home bases, have chosen to locate in "right-to-work" states and follow the nonunion model here. The labor strategy chosen by these producers, which had already penetrated the competitive U.S. market through imports and are globally as big as General Motors, raises the question of whether GM, and its unions, can survive. Reinforcing unionization in these core American industries involves directly taking on the recent entrants with new tools, such as corporate campaigns, to raise significantly the costs to employers of the antiunion model.

◆   *Targeting sectors of the economy, cities, or regions.* Union power rests not only on numbers. It also resides in the ability to leverage those numbers. The strategic application of union power has been integral to labor action from the beginning. But that ability changes as technology and the nature of the economy change. Coal miners once were able to bring factories to a close; they no longer can, anywhere in the world. Even as labor organizes new members, it should employ a directed and hard-nosed strategy to leverage its smaller numbers in the new global economy. In today's American economy, in certain sectors, such as transportation, communications, information, and product delivery, regional and large city labor markets are integral to the functioning of international commerce. Ensuring as close to 100 percent union density as feasible in those strategically vital areas should be a top priority for the American labor movement.

- *Redefining membership.* Throughout the 1980s, as membership dropped, the labor movement and others examined the potential for retaining links with *former* members, forging links with *potential* members, creating *associate* memberships and university and school programs. We encourage the labor movement to examine the ways in which membership may realistically be defined as something other than representation at the bargaining table. In particular, might there be a package of benefits—health, major medical, optical, dental, prepaid legal services, savings and pension/retirement options, housing finance, or child care—for which workers would associate with a union? While we do not contemplate that unions would cease to see their main function as representing workers in collective bargaining and enforcing the conditions negotiated, these attempts to move beyond the "job contract" as the basis for membership have met with success among retirees, and we think there is potential among other groups.

- *Developing a risk management strategy for organizing.* Unions argue that, ultimately, it pays for determined antiunion firms to delay and violate both the spirit and the letter of the law. In the early 1950s, about half a million workers unionized annually, with unions winning almost three-quarters of the elections held, and with contracts successfully resulting in 85 percent of the new bargaining units. By the late 1980s, annual unionization was down to about 80,000, with unions winning about half of the elections and only about half of those resulting in collective bargaining contracts. In addition, unions have been losing roughly two out of three elections to decertify them from representation.

  It should be anticipated that a sustained increase in organizing will bring with it a rise in the risks and costs borne by individual workers and by the unions themselves, in what has become a prolonged and contentious process. According to the AFL-CIO, a worker joining a union organizing campaign today faces about a one in eight chance of being fired; in 1995, at least 11,800 workers were dismissed while attempting to unionize. Many of these dismissed workers file complaints with the National Labor Relations Board. Under current law, while they await the Board's findings, they do not receive

unemployment compensation; they must find another job to
sustain themselves and their families. They lose income, health
coverage, and pension benefits and often end up relocating to
survive. The threat of dismissal and the lengthy justice process
represent hazardous obstacles in the path of workers seeking
to unionize.

These risks need to be addressed. **We suggest that the labor
movement experiment with an insurance-type plan to provide,
in a highly targeted way, interest-free loans to workers dismissed during organizing campaigns** (see Box 1). In addition to
fully compensating workers for lost income, such a plan would
motivate dismissed workers to file unfair labor practice charges,
would ensure a more stable workforce during a union organizing drive (by providing an incentive to remain through the
union representation vote), and might increase the cost to the
employer of illegally dismissing workers during organizing
campaigns. Such a plan would be expensive, with the estimat-
ed first-year cost of covering one hundred workers at $640,000
to $1 million, rising to $2.5 million to $4.5 million over five
years (see Box 1). Since the costs are highly sensitive to the
duration of dismissal, which is largely outside the control of the
worker or the union, we recommend a limited, pilot program,
which would also allow the labor movement to preserve solidarity by using its resources to cover all workers seeking unionization in a particular workplace.

2. Consolidate unions.

In facing the challenges of the new economy, there is much that
America's unions can learn from America's businesses, which have
understood the need to "adapt themselves" to the changed times.
One issue is organizational structure. There are too many unions;
many are very small. **Consolidation would conserve, mobilize, and
project strength, even before adding a single new member.** Bigger is
better because of economies of scale, which generate savings and servicing efficiencies. Also, whereas traditional union representation is
based on job title jurisdictions, more broadly based unions are better suited to deal strategically with rapid changes in technology and
skills and thus to help to improve U.S. competitiveness. Smaller
unions end up fighting rear guard, defensive, and tactical actions to

---

Box 1
A Proposed Insurance Plan: A Loan Covering One Hundred Workers Dismissed during Organizing Campaigns
Estimated Initial and Five-year Costs (1997 dollars)

	Income Replacement Rate = 100%	Income Replacement Rate = 80%	Income Replacement Rate = 60%
Year 1	$640,000	$512,000	$384,000
Year 3	416,900	333,500	250,100
Year 5	357,100	285,700	214,300
Total	$2,248,500	$1,798,800	$1,349100

ASSUMPTIONS:

1. Average duration of fifteen weeks, which represents a weighted average of recent NLRA cases.

2. Average weekly earnings before dismissal of $425 (in 1997 dollars).

3. Coverage of one hundred workers each year.

4. 25 percent of covered workers have their unfair labor charges dismissed and their loans forgiven.

5. 25 percent of covered workers reject the offer of reinstatement.

6. Workers rejecting offer of reinstatement are required to repay loan over five years.

7. Loan interest rate is zero.

8. Projected annual inflation = 2.7 percent for next five years, from U.S. government budget estimates.

9. Workers accepting reinstatement receive average back pay award = half of lost wages. (Assumes back pay award = 1.5 x lost wages minus expected wage income [if employed] = 2/3 x previous wage.)

10. For workers accepting reinstatement: loan repayment = back pay awarded (if award is less than the loan); if award is greater than the loan, worker repays total loan.

Note: The cost estimates here are highly sensitive to the duration of the loan (identical to duration of dismissal). For example, if we assume average duration in a range of 50 percent below and 50 percent above the weighted average of fifteen weeks, the first-year costs for the plan at 100 percent income replacement are $318,750 and $956,250 respectively, with the total five-year costs running as low as $1.124 million or as high as $3.4 million. Further, if dismissal duration were to be double that assumed in the above table, total five-year costs could run as high as $4.5 million per one hundred workers.

Thanks to Helena Jorgensen, Department of Public Policy, AFL-CIO, for the calculations and research underlying the assumptions in this model.

---

protect their own base. Unfortunately, union mergers, like those in business, confront and often collapse under the weight of very personal issues: protecting incumbents; eliminating duplicate or redundant operations; advancing or sidelining certain individuals. Overcoming these issues quickly and efficiently should be the order of the day. We are struck by the experiences of the Steelworkers and of the Union of Needletrades, Industrial and Textile Employees (UNITE!), in their mergers and efforts to reorganize themselves, including the amalgamation of small, local unions into larger ones, which seems to offer living proof that this path results in stronger, more efficacious unions. We look forward to a rapid and successful merger of the present steel, auto, and machinists' unions into a streamlined and effective union of American metalworkers.

The other issue involves resources and financing. The American union structure resembles a pyramid: the base (local unions) collects and keeps 70 percent of the resources largely for contract-related issues, and the other 30 percent flows up to the international unions, the state, the regional, and the national federation. We note that if the AFL-CIO is to coordinate and use such a decentralized set of resources in the huge, sustained effort necessary to rebuild membership, it will likely require significant changes in governance, dues, and board representation. This will need to be accompanied by an education campaign among dues-paying members and their local unions.

3. Change labor's response to heightened global economic competition by promoting unions as an asset in the workplace.

In industry after industry, including automobiles, steel, airlines, and basic transportation, individual companies struggling to meet heightened competition have turned to their unions for infusions of capital and increased participation in production and investment decisions. Even in the absence of crisis, involving workers and their unions in workplace decisions brings to bear the expertise they have about their jobs and should raise productivity. Numerous studies indicate that unions increase productivity in the following ways: by inducing greater investment in technology, by increasing training, by lowering employee turnover, and by requiring more professional management. Further, detailed examinations of particular workplaces indicate that the impact of unions on productivity depends not only on what union or management does separately but also on their relationship with one another. In short, higher productivity appears to go together with good industrial relations.

Heightened global competition raises the stakes of shop-floor cooperation considerably. Yet, the benefits and the success stories, while no surprise to unionized firms, are little known and rarely broadcast to the community at large. With the shrinking of the unionized private sector, unions can no longer assume that the public understands what they are about. There are two distinct challenges. One is to get the story out. To the public in general, the message is that high-performance workplaces work best when there is a union. Toward members, though, unions must wage a more sophisticated campaign. They must educate members that, while there is a role for cooperation in bringing the enterprise up to the technology and productivity standards of the twenty-first century, the potential for conflict remains when it becomes necessary to protect the union's existence and hard-won wage and benefit gains.

The other challenge is to find new models and other venues to improve worker productivity. Several task force members cited a range of regional and industry-specific partnerships, where unions and employers, sometimes linked with secondary schools and community colleges, have formed nonprofit organizations to improve productivity, workplace cooperation, and industrial performance. These partnerships serve as employment centers—by training, screening, and placing employees with state-of-the-art skills—or they function as information centers on changing technology and best practices for small and medium-sized enterprises in specific industries. Examples of such new models are the New York City Garment Industry Development Corporation, founded in 1984; the Wisconsin Regional Training Partnership, focused on the durable goods sector; the Andrew J. Gress Graphic Arts Institute, linked to new technology in the printing industry; Oregon's Partners in Construction Cooperation; Pittsburgh's Steel Valley Authority; the Seattle Worker Center; and the San Francisco Hotels Partnership. These all seem promising, and, in the spirit of creativity, we encourage such experiments.

4. Meet the changing geography of the modern corporation with new global alliances and international action.

Globalization has changed the economic rules and diffused power among nation-states, markets, corporations, unions, and workers. For years American unions focused on domestic labor law and collective bargaining relationships with U.S. corporations to produce a rising standard of living for American workers. Now, when location decisions are determined by the global movement of investment capital and technology, the contract and the law are often made irrelevant. Into this more diffused and decentralized world economy, unions bring an outdated and hierarchical form of transnational organization. Local, plant-level unions rarely have global connection at all. Until fairly recently, cross-national links among unions have formed only at the highest levels and centered on events affecting an entire industry— through International Trade Secretariats (ITS)—and on issues raised at the multilateral institutions, particularly the UN's International Labor Organization and the Organization for Economic Cooperation and Development. These organizations are remote and opaque, especially from the viewpoint of the local union. Unfortunately, unions rarely organized themselves transnationally by corporate employer and now find themselves significantly behind the curve.

Even as international labor institutions have become sclerotic, nongovernmental organizations—covering the environment, human rights, women's rights, and poverty alleviation—have used cutting-edge technology to form global networks that attempt to raise public consciousness, inform the policy debate, and take legal action on a range of global issues. These groups offer the labor movement models, support, and potential allies in gearing up for a different world of labor action. The AFL-CIO must actively encourage member unions that bargain with multinational corporations to forge horizontal, working relationships with all of their worldwide counterparts on a company-by-company basis. In addition, given the low union density in the United States, American unions should embark on a strategy to (1) leverage the greater strength of unions around the world in furthering their aims; (2) focus on the global performance, employment, and technology strategies of particular corporations; and (3) forge tactical alliances with business groups and NGOs on issues of common concern, such as the use of child and prison labor, discriminatory employment practices, and the undermining of effective standard setting and market regulation through corrupt practices.

5. Use politics and public policy to regain standing in a hostile public arena.

Political clout reflects union membership and density. As these dwindle, unions are forced to push harder to deliver for their existing members, often on narrowly focused concerns, just at the time when they need to widen appeal to nonmembers and work more cooperatively in coalition with other groups. Increasingly, unions represent people who experience the workplace differently from most workers. If they modernize their political vocabulary to fit the prevailing work environment, will their members think they are doing the right job? If they do not modernize, how can they appeal to the majority of America's workers?

This is the dilemma of leadership that unions face. Members pay dues and members vote. It takes enlightened leadership to convince them that their dues, their staff, and their organization should be working hard on behalf of nonmembers and non-dues-payers. This is especially difficult to do around officer election time. To move forward, the leadership must come from the top of the unions and from the AFL-CIO. In short, the union leadership must lead powerfully.

The primary vehicle to broaden the appeal of unions is to raise labor's voice on a range of issues important to all workers, unionized or not. Politics and public policy offer the stage on which to exercise that voice in the interests of all working people, promoting legislation to improve their well-being. This will require a well-thought-out strategy to marshal resources by building permanent alliances for an agenda promoting a fair distribution of the economic pie and by choosing the political/legislative fights carefully. The fight to raise the minimum wage is a prime example of such a strategy, although judgment is not yet in on whether it was used to build and cement permanent alliances within a wider, progressive community. We think child care, family leave, and quality health care are likely to be others.

Clearly, there is a tough road ahead; it ought not to be traveled in isolation. As workplace institutions, unions will help business to ensure a competitive American economy in the twenty-first century. As a countervailing force for workers seeking a fair share of the economic pie, unions help society to preserve a rising standard of living for American families. In addition, unions play an important citizenship role that the country is in danger of losing. Laying out a new social compact was beyond our mission, but this country needs something along those lines. Social compacts derive their authority and durability from the strength and standing that each constituency brings to the table. We are convinced that it is time for corporate America, government, and civic institutions to recognize the stake that society has in a revitalized and strong labor movement. We offer our recommendations on ways in which America's unions can help themselves as a means of encouraging a larger, societywide dialogue on labor's future. For if America's unions fail in the task of rebuilding themselves, all Americans will lose.

STATEMENT OF NELSON LICHTENSTEIN

The task force report asserts the value of U.S. trade unionism, both in defending the living standards of the American people and in energizing participatory democracy itself. That The Century Foundation makes such an assertion is a signal accomplishment, given unions' raison d'etre standing against the unfettered play of a "free" market that, in our post–cold war era, too many policymakers and pundits see as synonymous with democracy itself. The report therefore represents a proud, if partial, return to the vision of Twentieth Century Fund founder Edward Filene, who played such an important role early in this century as a tireless advocate for a union-centered system of "industrial democracy."

But this report requires even greater boldness to explain why a labor renaissance is essential to the health of American democracy and how that might be accomplished. For if the labor movement is to make inroads among those who work in the new information-age economy, the trade unions will need to engineer a political and cultural breakthrough that sways the hearts and minds of millions and millions of people who today see the unions as irrelevant, or even hostile, to their interests. The AFL-CIO organizing posture today is an aggressive one because federation leaders understand that if they wish to organize 300,000 new workers each year—which is the number required merely to maintain union density at its current level—then the unions must once again transform themselves into a social movement (as happened during those brief moments of explosive growth—in the 1880s, during the first decade of the twentieth century, amid the Great Depression, and throughout the 1960s among many public service workers) and in the process begin a reconfiguration of the American political landscape itself.

Thus, the preconditions for the nation's era of union rebirth will be set not by a better understanding of how these institutions contribute to economic efficiency, productivity enhancement, or even to political pluralism, important as those phenomena may be. Rather, a union renaissance will take place when having a rights-conscious industrial democracy is once again moved to the top of the nation's social agenda, when the reorganization of office, factory, and store is no longer the presumptive monopoly of management and its propagandists but once again takes its place as a vital subject of public policy, popular consciousness, and classwide insurgency. This is not the same thing as "voice" or "participation"—the terms themselves are deracinated social science—but instead is a matter of democracy, solidarity, and workplace power. This was the mission to which Edward Filene devoted his money and his talents in the years leading up to the passage of the Wagner Act, and it must become the task of many of those opinion leaders to whom this report is addressed, both inside the AFL-CIO and out.

To rebuild themselves, the unions, and those who seek to advance their fortunes, need to take two ideas more seriously. The first is solidarity, a concept that is usually associated with strike militancy, inspiring songs, and raised fists. Such tactics still have value, but here I want to highlight the continuing importance of a broad and inclusive workers' movement in an era when globalization, corporate reorganizations, and rapid technological change put labor and product markets in a constant state of flux. In telecommunications, the merger of Nynex, Bell Atlantic, and GTE has completely shaken up the internal labor market of this new information-age corporation. In the once stable auto industry, GM's spin-off of its Delphi parts division is throwing more than 50,000 senior workers into a world of low-wage, nonunion production. And Chrysler workers, who once thought they labored for a highly profitable, highly efficient U.S. firm, now find themselves linked to the fortunes of a German manufacturer whose overcapacity is worrisome.

Such postmodern, postindustrial transformations have devalued both the Wagner-era idea of collective bargaining within a single firm or factory and the more recent managerial effort to enhance work-site competitiveness through programs of "team" production and "flexible" job redefinition. Whatever the merits of either system, their worth erodes dramatically in an era of such rapid transmutations in the structure of the firm, the market, and the technology. Productivity rises rapidly, but there is no guarantee that its fruits will be distributed in an equitable fashion. Under these conditions, a recommitment to the solidarity of labor, to a politicized, classwide union movement, is essential to reduce job insecurity, temper each cycle of wage competition, and recast technological innovation from a threat to an opportunity.

Solidarity is not a product of organizational discipline but individual activity on the part of the worker. The task force report ignores entirely the question of internal union democracy, or rather of those institutional and administrative obstacles that stand in the way of an empowered and alert membership. Union democracy is not a luxury, an ethical imperative divorced from the hard work necessary to rebuild the movement. Instead, it stands at the very center of that rebuilding process. The unions need tens of thousands of new organizers, but the AFL-CIO cannot recruit, train, and deploy such an army, and even if it could, "organizers" who parachute into a campaign are far less effective than those who are part of the community and the workplace. But such homegrown cadres cannot be recruited in the absence of a democratic, participatory union culture. Unfortunately, thousands of local unions, and not a few national or international organizations, are job trusts that exist to protect the incomes of an entrenched stratum of long-serving officials. The democratization of the union movement threatens the security and prerogatives of these men and women, but without that maturation the union movement will remain a shell.

The task force should therefore call upon the top officials of the AFL-CIO to encourage union democracy in all its forms. Among the changes this might require are the following: an end to restrictive qualifications on those who wish to run for union office; the election of shop stewards and business agents by the membership on a regular basis; the election of top union officials by referendum vote; the posting of contracts proposed for ratification on union web pages; and, in all union business, the routine dissemination of minority as well as majority reports.

Cynics will write off much of the above as impractical or romantic, but the most notable trade union victory of our times was largely based on just such a program. The Teamster success in the 1997 United Parcel Service strike demonstrated that democracy, militancy, and the generation of a movement culture paid off handsomely. A vigorous reform movement within the Teamsters opened the door to a mass mobilization that proved the key to victory in the strike. The demand for more full-time jobs proved popular with both working Teamsters and would-be scabs, but of equal importance was the union determination and internal coherence that had been built during years of struggle with United Parcel

Service. A critical issue here was the rejection of the team concept schemes put forward by UPS and other trucking companies. As the union slogan put it: "We already have a Team—it's called the Teamsters." This multiyear struggle against the shipping firm's effort to erode union solidarity built the cadre necessary to put backbone into the 1997 picket lines and demonstrate to the tens of thousands of potential strikebreakers—and to the public at large— that the Teamsters Union, and not UPS, had their best interests at heart.

STATEMENT OF CHARLES HECKSCHER

This report reflects the task force's hope for a revival of the labor movement as an effective force for employee representation. All of us share a deep sense of alarm at the breakdown of the old social compact and the increase in wage disparity of the past twenty years. The United States was built from its inception on careful balances of power; today, that balance, at least in employment, is clearly out of whack. Employers in many industries can act without concern for anyone but their own shareholders, and neither labor nor government has the might to stand up to them. As a result, employees have suffered in terms of declining real wages and growing insecurity, while gains have gone disproportionately to corporations, their top managers, and their shareholders.

By drawing a simple link between the decline of labor and the rise of inequality, however, the report blurs the enormous social and economic changes that underlie the shift in power. It implies that a simple revival of the labor movement would solve the problem. Yet there are many indications that changes in the society and economy are so deep that the old labor movement could not deal with them—that what is needed is a *new* labor movement.

At their height unions were seen as a key part of a system that brought strength and prosperity to the whole nation. They contributed to the economy by providing labor stability and increased purchasing power, and they were a vital part of the politically dominant New Deal coalition. That is not the case today. Though in the abstract unions are widely viewed as necessary, concretely they are generally seen as outdated and defensive, as drains on productivity, as narrowly self-interested. This is the reason, I think, for the confusing poll findings mentioned in the report.

Essentially the polls show that people want unions but not the unions we have now. They want a counterweight to corporate power but one that will contribute to economic growth and dynamism. There is a tremendous appetite for effective representation of a new sort. That implies that unions have to change substantially in order to play their designated role in the current economy.

There are at least three huge changes that, while deeply threatening, could also form the foundation "pillars" for a rebuilding of labor—though not without considerable redesign as well as rebuilding. First, there is the rise of new movements and of employment rights. Most of the advances in workplace justice in the thirty years leading to today have come not from traditional labor action but from the driving energy of blacks, women, gays, the disabled, and other such social identity groups. Despite the very considerable backlash of conservative forces, these social networks retain their vitality. The Americans with Disabilities Act, passed in this decade with bipartisan congressional support and signed by a Republican president, has established a pivotal new requirement that companies make reasonable accommodation to the needs of one category of employees.

Labor has supported many of these movements—playing an important role in the passage of the Civil Rights Act and most of its extensions—but has never succeeded in forming a unified and stable alliance with them. More than fifteen years ago, the "Solidarity Day" march tried to bring together a broad range of social action causes, but the solidarity quickly faded. All parties have tended to focus on their own issues and to demand particular rights rather than seeking common ground. In order for labor to make good its potential as a natural leader of these forces, it has to frame a social vision that fully includes them.

A second area of fundamental change is in employment mobility. Economic studies have recently begun to document what was widely felt intuitively: that job tenures have declined and mobility has increased. Contingent work—temporary, part time, and contract—by most measures now represents more than 30 percent of the employment picture.

There is a tendency for labor and its supporters simply to try to stop this increased mobility through restrictions on employers. But this misses two essential points: first, there is a general belief that businesses need increased flexibility in order to innovate and remain dynamic; the high unemployment rate in the European social democracies seems persuasive evidence that regulation does not help employees overall. Second, many employees, particularly younger ones, want the opportunity for entrepreneurial independence.

There are some labor strategies that move into new territory, trying to create a framework for real mobility. Currently, mobility is held back by the fact that employees have no support in the open market: when they lose jobs they also lose health benefits and pensions, as well as psychological support and a sense of meaning and community; moreover, they have little access to good financial advice, knowledge about new career opportunities, continuing education—all the elements that would make a truly mobile system work. There is no real reason, other than tradition and habit, why the labor movement cannot supply many of these things and in so doing build a reputation for enhancing economic growth and employee opportunity rather than restricting them.

A third basic shift is in the internal structure of companies. For decades they have been struggling to reduce bureaucratic rigidity and increase participation, decentralizing their structures, encouraging teamwork, and rewarding people according to their contribution to the overall mission. There is little doubt that such changes increase competitiveness. Labor has been ambivalent: though some unions have been involved in major participatory efforts (especially in steel, automobiles, and telecommunications), many resist decentralization because it undercuts unified bargaining, reject differentiated rewards because they violate solidarity, and balk at teamwork because it leads inevitably to the breaking of traditional contractual rules.

Again, it would be possible to make a virtue of the dangers by positioning labor as the champion of genuine participation. The rhetoric of management and the evidence both suggest that true participation is good for the economy as well as workers, yet in most cases it is implemented by companies in a very limited and grudging way. After all, managers, too, are reluctant to give up their familiar ways of acting and to leap into an abyss of the unknown. If they are not challenged, they will naturally try to go halfway, talking participation and teamwork without really changing very much. Unions could try making a priority of developing a strong model of participation to pressure employers to live up to their own rhetoric.

Mobility and participation are two aspects of the competitiveness debate that now dominates our national discourse. There is a compelling case to be made that labor can increase competitiveness, just as it boosted the economy in the 1930s by increasing purchasing power.

In brief, I am suggesting that the employment system has to fit with current economic and social needs, and in order to do this, it must unambivalently work with rather than against the basic changes that have transformed our workplaces and culture. The labor movement should be a leader in seeking individual and civil rights, in building a society that is safe for mobility and entrepreneurship, and in demanding real participation that fully utilizes the intelligence and creativity of employees.

The rub is that in order to realize this vision the labor movement has to reinvent itself radically, moving away from its traditional focus on protection of jobs and work rules. I do not think there is a definitive blueprint for how to do that. This is a period for experimentation. There are in fact a great many creative experiments under way—regional economic strategies, union-based temp agencies, joint training and placement mechanisms, labor-led civil rights suits, minority caucuses, unionized, worker-owned companies—the list could go on for pages. Many of these efforts are occurring within the AFL-CIO; others are based outside it.

The inability of this task force to agree on recommendations suggests that instead of a set of proposals we should structure dialogue around this widened scope. At the moment different groups striving for workplace justice are fragmented; those that lie outside the AFL-CIO, instead of flocking to it for its centralized strength, are largely keeping their distance, worried that organized labor will stifle them. For that reason labor cannot build a coalition for change by itself. An organization like The Century Foundation could play a valuable role in hosting discussions among these natural allies.

To confront the current challenges, labor and its allies need to clear the air through conversing about shared goals and to reach a common vision—a vision of an employment system that furthers competitiveness, accountability, and flexibility as well as the timeless goals of security, equity, and community.

Background Paper

by Nelson Lichtenstein

AMERICAN TRADE UNIONS AND THE "LABOR QUESTION": PAST AND PRESENT

E ighty years ago "the labor question" stood at the center of American social and political consciousness. Even before the nation's most massive, sustained strike wave convulsed every industrial district in 1919, President Woodrow Wilson cabled from Versailles:

> The question which stands at the front of all others amidst the present great awakening is the question of labor . . . how are the men and women who do the daily labor of the world to obtain progressive improvement in the conditions of their labor, to be made happier, and to be served better by the communities and the industries which their labor sustains and advances.[1]

In the decades that followed President Wilson's missive, the "labor question" seemed well on its way to resolution. The labor law reforms of the New Deal era, the rise of a powerful trade union movement, the prosperity of the postwar era, and the growth of an innovative culture of personal management and organizational exper- imentation seemed to promise that the "labor question" would soon transform itself into a technically manageable subdiscipline in which issues of "collective bargaining," "industrial relations," "personnel management," "workplace restructuring," and "team production" were the province of academic, administrative, and judicial experts.

THE CURRENT IMPASSE

But the "labor question" has come roaring back at the end of the twentieth century. Tepid productivity growth, decades of wage stagnation, job insecurity, a dramatic decline in union strength punctuated by the occasional violent (lost) strike demonstrate that the issues that once confronted Progressive Era reformers like Woodrow Wilson are with us still. During the long economic recovery that characterized the 1990s, the U.S. economy grew by almost 3 percent each year, but for most of that era the median income of American households suffered a continuous annual decline. Thus, by the late 1990s, real household income for young families (breadwinners under age thirty) stood at one-third less than that of their counterparts in 1973, even though their total working hours were longer and the educational level attained by the head of household was higher than a generation before. By 1996 median wages and family incomes were still below their 1989 level.[2]

Indeed, virtually all efforts to spark real wage growth and negotiate a consensual reform of the American workplace have come to an impasse during the past few years, even when backed by influential corporate executives, top trade unionists, numerous elected officials, and the White House. During the first two years of the Clinton administration a remarkably ambitious set of reforms was put in play, but almost every initiative collapsed in the face of internal division and paralyzing opposition. Programs to stimulate school-to-work transitions, infrastructure construction, on-the-job training, and strategic industrial planning floundered during the early years of the administration even as it commanded Democratic majorities in both houses of Congress.

The failure of the administration's elaborately crafted health security initiative proved particularly devastating, for this program was one of the most ambitious and long-overdue pieces of social legislation put on the national agenda since the New Deal. Although the Clintons and their many advisers sought to orchestrate a grand compromise that would accommodate the divergent interests of just about every player within the health care political economy, their effort collapsed in such a dramatic fashion that it threatened Social Security, undermined Aid to Families with Dependent Children, and put in jeopardy other venerable bulwarks of the American welfare state.[3] Shaken by these defeats, the Clinton administration soon deemphasized the growth of wage inequality and the stagnation of living standards, which had been important themes during much of its first term. In their place administration officials adopted a defensive, minimalist social program; indeed, President Clinton conducted his successful 1996 reelection campaign by claiming that deficit reduction, combined with Reaganesque levels of job growth and unemployment, actually constituted a fulfillment of his political mandate.[4]

The union movement has had a particularly difficult time reestablishing a sense of legitimacy and functionality within both the political economy and the microsocial world of workplace governance. The argument made by economists Richard Freedman and Barry Bluestone, and by most trade union leaders—that unionism generates positive employment effects: lowering quit rates, raising job tenure, as well as increasing productivity and skill levels—has won little assent in the corporate world, perhaps not unexpectedly at a time when many managers celebrate the "virtual corporation" and declare that a sense of merely contingent and temporary attachment to the firm represents the most technologically congruent, culturally sophisticated industrial relations policy. Management efforts to avoid or eliminate trade unionism hardly weakened as the Reaganite 1980s gave way to a new decade and a new administration. Bitter, union-breaking lockout strikes at the *Detroit Free Press*, Caterpillar, Bridgestone-Firestone, and Yale University testified to management self-confidence and the institutional fragility of the contemporary labor movement. Even the notable 1997 Teamster victory at United Parcel Service did little to reverse the antiunion tide. Although tens of thousands of unionists and their backers successfully mobilized much popular support against the nationwide corporation, the Teamster success at UPS generated no sea change in management thinking and few organizing ripples in other industrial or service sectors of the economy.

Indeed, even under the benign chairmanship of John Dunlop, a former secretary of labor, the high-profile "Commission on the Future of Worker-Management Relations" could find little common ground, other than the purely rhetorical, that might enable progressive employers and incrementalist unions, to say nothing of their more adversarial-minded counterparts, to reach agreement on the kind of labor law reform needed to sustain trade union organization, facilitate genuine employee participation, and advance even a minimal sort of "voice" for unorganized workers. Dunlop, AFL-CIO leaders, and many in the administration had hoped to strike a new social bargain. The unions would agree to a revision of Section 8(a)(2) of the National Labor Relations Act (NLRA, also known as the Wagner Act), banning company unions, after which companies would have a free hand to set up management-run employee participation committees. In return the trade union movement would win long-overdue labor law reforms—chiefly the "card check," which would allow unions to secure quick, formal certification when a majority of workers sign authorization cards—designed to make organizing easier. But such a deal collapsed even before the Republicans captured control of Congress for the first time in forty years. Labor remained suspicious that legally sanctioned employee participation schemes represented little more than a new form of union avoidance, while no significant segment of the business community was willing to countenance the renewed growth of trade unionism, whatever the quid pro quo.[5]

This stalemate has had many causes, but the key to them all is the unprecedented weakness of the American trade union movement. Its demise over the past quarter-century is now a dismal and oft-told story, but the statistical record bears one more brief review. At the end of the twentieth century, the 15 million organized workers represent less than 16 percent of the entire nonfarm workforce; in the private sector, not quite 11 percent. This means that unions in the United States represent a lower proportion of the workforce than in any other industrial democracy in the world. If 1953 is taken as the proportional apogee of U.S. trade unionism in this century, then organized labor is only one-third as strong today as it was forty years ago, only a quarter as strong in the private sector. In no industry does the trade union movement represent even half of all employees: even in the automobile industry, once the flagship of American labor, the parts sector is more than 80 percent nonunion, while most of the German and Japanese transplants are also unorganized. Given such weakness, unionists have shelved the strike weapon. In 1995 there were only thirty-one strikes, involving more than one thousand workers; twenty years before there had been ten times as many.[6]

Today, union activism—at the bargaining table, the ballot box, and on the picket line—is almost always designed to defend the status quo. Union efforts to preserve jobs and wage structures are the near universal subject of most major collective bargaining negotiations. Union contract settlements, even in the seventh year of an economic recovery, barely keep up with inflation; by 1996 the share of national income going to wages was at its lowest level in almost three decades. Meanwhile, company efforts to cut health care costs (and benefits) generate more than two-thirds of all the strikes that do take place.[7]

This background paper is therefore predicated upon the idea that a larger and more powerful trade union movement is essential to any progressive resolution of the contemporary stalemate that structures social politics in the United States, with an eye not only to wage stagnation and underemployment but also to the persistence of gender inequality, the rightward drift in American politics, and most important, the nation's chronic racial divide. The paper reviews several decades of trade union history, paying particular attention to those ideological and structural issues that seem to have some resonance today; to wit, an examination of the sources of union growth in the 1930s and 1960s and of the alternative programs once advanced by proponents and opponents of a reconstructed industrial relations system in the mid-century years, a somewhat revisionist reading of what has now come to be known as the era of the labor-management accord (1947–78), a discussion of the new turn in corporate and governmental labor relations after 1978, and an assessment of the trade union movement's difficulties during the era of Ronald Reagan and after.

UNION GROWTH IN THE 1930S

Among contemporary unionists, managers, and industrial relations practitioners, a programmatically convenient, contemporary mythology has emerged to explain both the dramatic growth of the labor movement in the New Deal era and the seeming irrelevance of the union idea to our own era. Those who look with equanimity upon the demise of the unions late in the twentieth

century imagine an unbridgeable divide separating fin de siècle
America from the economic structures of the Depression decade
and from a factory technology characterized by the complete dom-
inance of a mass production regime. Management thinking today
declares unions "irrelevant" because they no longer play a useful
function, either for workers or capitalists, in our computer-driven,
postindustrial, post-Fordism world. The AFL-CIO and its allies
are committed to the revival of the unions in the twenty-first century, but these embattled laborites have often constructed an equally implausible master narrative. They wistfully recall an era when
the New Deal state seemed to stand solidly on their side, when the
Wagner Act—dubbed "Labor's Magna Carta"—effectively protected organizing rights, and when industrial workers battled for
union recognition with one voice and one fist.[8]

A closer look at what actually happened in the 1930s and
1940s demonstrates that the issues faced by unionists, policymakers, and corporate managers were hardly irrelevant to our own
times. Trade unionism moved to the center of the political agenda
during the 1930s because the state-assisted growth of this institution seemed to offer solutions to two of the critical problems confronting the early twentieth century political economy. The first
was "underconsumption," a concept whose most active popularizer
was undoubtedly Twentieth Century Fund founder Edward Filene.
"Cutthroat" pricing and relative wage decline in the 1920s had
destabilized American capitalism and transformed a Wall Street
panic into a worldwide depression. Individual employers wanted
prices to stabilize and wages to rise, but only for their competitors. The solution therefore was a broad, upward shift in working-
class purchasing power, a Keynesian prescription that made the
interests of the new unions, the only prospective institution then
capable of policing a revision of industrywide wage standards,
largely synonymous with those of the nation.[9]

But if the trade unions were successful only as wage-fixing
institutions, their appeal would have diminished considerably
among policymaking elites still seeking a resolution of the vio-
lence-plagued "labor question" and, even more decisively, among
the mass of American workers, a huge proportion of them of
immigrant or African-American stock, for whom the New Deal
and the new unionism represented a doorway that opened onto

the democratic promise of American life. The Wagner Act was a radical legislative initiative because it sought to democratize the world of work in order to counterbalance the "industrial autocracy" that had been the preoccupation of both Progressive reformers and left-wing insurgents since the 1880s. New Deal labor legislation was designed to put in place a permanent set of institutions, situated within the very womb of private enterprise, that offered workers a voice, and sometimes a club, with which to resolve their grievances and organize themselves for economic struggle and collective political action.

Collective bargaining, wrote Harvard's Sumner Slichter, then dean of American labor economists, is a method of "introducing civil rights into industry, that is, of requiring that management be conducted by rule rather than by arbitrary decision." To Slichter and many of the interwar generation, "industrial jurisprudence" represented far more than the employee "voice" that contemporary industrial relations experts see as a key to enhanced productivity. Slichter made that argument as well in the 1930s, but to the men and women of his academic generation, collective bargaining represented a new normative social order: it was both a technique of conflict resolution and an effort to establish a new constitutionalism within American factories and mills. "Before organization came into the plant, foremen were little tin gods in their own departments," declared a 1941 UAW steward's handbook. "With the coming of the union, the foreman finds his whole world turned upside down. His small time dictatorship has been overthrown, and he must be adjusted to a democratic system of shop government."[10]

These two elements of New Deal industrial relations policy were mutually reinforcing. The new unions of the 1930s and 1940s played a decisive role in transforming an immigrant, industrial "peasantry" into an organized body of social citizens whose political weight reshaped the American polity for two generations. In this sense the industrial union movement of the 1930s—and to some extent the civil rights movement of two decades later—played the same role in the United States as did the rise of social democratic parties in Europe at the turn of the century. It has been a truism in social science scholarship that the American working class was "exceptional" because it won the franchise before the rise of industrial capitalism, one reason for the weakness of both institutional unionism and socialist ideology in this country.[11] But for at least half of the pre–New Deal industrial working class—not only African Americans but immigrants from Southern and Eastern Europe as well—the right to vote was pure formalism, underutilized or unavailable until well into the twentieth century.

Indeed, it was the union movement and the New Deal that advanced a powerful sense of culturally pluralist citizenship. By giving first- and second-generation immigrant workers a collective political voice, transforming power relations at the work site and compressing wage scales that all too often mirrored invidious ethnic and racial hierarchies, CIO-style industrial unionism offered the New Deal a solid material foundation upon which to advance a socially inclusive redefinition of mid-century citizenship. "Unionism is the spirit of Americanism," asserted a typical union paper that spoke for second-generation immigrant workers. In western Pennsylvania steel towns and New England textile centers, the new citizenship and the new unionism were virtually synonymous, thus linking union vigor, voter participation, political power, and income growth in a virtuous circle. The Roosevelt landslides of the 1930s were a product not of Republican crossover voters (African Americans were the big exception here) but of the Democratic Party's success in mobilizing a whole stratum of once-alienated immigrant "un-Americans" into an electoral coalition that dominated politics for the next thirty years. From 1932 to 1948 the class difference between the electoral base of the Democrats and of the Republicans became increasingly pronounced. Indeed, by 1948 the proportion of American working-class voters who cast ballots for the Democrats was as high as that of their British Labour Party counterparts.[12]

Of course, this system was hardly consensual. Whatever the economic and political logic of New Deal unionism, the new regime never achieved the kind of legitimacy found in Northern Europe after the war. American business came to terms with the new unionism only with the greatest reluctance. As Ezra Vogel and Sanford Jacoby have pointed out, the most "exceptional" element in the American system of labor-management relations is the hostility managers have shown toward both the regulatory state and virtually all systems of worker representation. Their response reflected both an ideological commitment to a set of entrepreneurial prerogatives and the relatively decentralized, competitive structure of many of the most important industries. Thus, the cartelization implicit in the National Recovery Administration effort at industry self-governance had collapsed by 1935, even before the Supreme Court declared such a regulatory scheme unconstitutional. And, despite much wishful historiography, no well-organized "corporate liberal" cohort of enlightened businessmen supported either the Wagner Act or the Social Security Act.[13]

Nor was there much unity within the world of labor. The Rooseveltian reform of labor relations was based upon a working class that was no more homogeneous than that of our own time. Nearly all of the recent social histories of this era emphasize the fierce ethnoreligious fissures that confronted union organizers and energized the political conflicts splintering so many unions. There were "culture wars" in the 1930s, too. The great rivalry that divided the American Federation of Labor (AFL) and the Congress of Industrial Organizations (CIO) was based not only on their celebrated dispute over the craft versus the industrial form of organization but more fundamentally upon the disdain with which so many in the AFL hierarchy greeted the industrially organized immigrants comprising the bulk of the workers in steel, packinghouses, and automobile manufacturing. Much of the AFL was rooted in the Protestant lower-middle class and the old labor aristocracy of northern European descent. These men and women had a substantial stake in the old order, be it the comfortable politics of a small Midwestern town or the chance to climb a few steps higher within the workplace hierarchy. Through the Masons, the Knights of Columbus, the evangelical churches, through kinship and friendship, they had forged a hundred and one social and cultural links with those who were more solidly bourgeois. In the early 1930s, when the whole social structure seemed on the verge of collapse, these plebeian elites had swung into the ambit of corporatist radicals like Huey Long, Upton Sinclair, and Father Coughlin, whose economic radicalism was matched by a profound social and cultural conservatism.

But the industrial unions mobilized, organized, and gave voice to that huge mass that had stood just below, or just outside, the social structures this more established working class stratum saw as its own. The CIO made shop-floor citizens of Eastern European Catholics, African Americans, French Canadians, and migratory Appalachians whose relationship to the old German, Irish, and northern Protestant elite had been one of deference and subordination. Moreover the CIO, with its leaven of radical Jews and anti-clerical Catholics and its rationalizing, modernizing, and cosmopolitan outlook, threatened the lifetime of social capital and ethnic privilege built up by those whose outlooks were more parochial and insular. No wonder that the late 1930s saw a recrudescence of right-wing agitation and red-baiting wherever the new unions disrupted the old order. Thus, the terrorist Black Legion flourished in Pontiac and Flint and the KKK at Packard and at other auto assembly plants in Indiana, Missouri, and Texas. Company-sponsored vigilante groups had little difficulty winning recruits in either California agribusiness or the industrial towns of upstate New York and New England. All this helps explain not only the continuance of the AFL-CIO wars well into the 1940s (including an AFL penchant for allying itself with employers to forestall CIO organizing efforts) but also the epidemic of factionalism that fractured CIO unions in the electrical, farm equipment, automobile, and lumber industries.[14]

If this troubled history serves to demolish the convenient but mythic imagery of labor solidarity in the 1930s, it may have much contemporary usefulness. Although the cultural and racial fissures break along different lines today, union organizers confront a working class that is no more homogeneous than that of sixty years ago. The difference then between an Anglo-Gaelic tool-and-die maker at Ford's giant River Rouge complex outside Detroit and a first-generation Hungarian assembler in Cleveland was just about the same in terms of training and outlook as that between a Microsoft programmer in Seattle and a data entry homeworker in Omaha. In the 1930s, as in the 1990s, unionism in the needle trades required the harmonization of a bewildering array of immigrant ethnic particularisms; likewise, the entrenched racial and occupational hierarchies in construction, health care, and municipal service require as much attention today as in the past. The unionization process does not demand homogeneity in either skill, ethnicity, or language. Instead, it requires a compelling set of ideas and the institutions, both social and governmental, to give labor's cause power and legitimacy. "Class consciousness," wrote E. P. Thompson, is "made," not "given."[15]

This understanding of the great obstacles that faced the framers of New Deal labor law and the leaders of the new unionism is important because it bears directly upon the contemporary controversy over revision of NLRA's Section 8(a)(2), which proscribes employer-dominated "company unions," whose modern heir is the employee involvement or team production committee. The Wagner Act's rather definitive opposition to such employer-instigated workplace institutions arose out of much experience with them, especially in the years just after World War I and in the early 1930s when, in industries like steel, rubber, and electrical products, they seemed to have acquired considerable legitimacy. They did provide an element of "voice," and in a 1934 effort to maintain industry cooperation with the recovery effort, President Roosevelt appointed a series of labor boards that practically endorsed them. In later years several such company representation plans—at DuPont and TRW, for example—detached themselves from management just enough so that they fell under the coverage of the new labor law as real—if weak—trade unions. Not unexpectedly, all union leaders, as well as the principal authors of the Wagner Act, successfully argued for an absolute ban on such company-sponsored unions because they contended that such institutions would merely perpetuate managerial power and exacerbate the deep divisions within the workforce. An ersatz democracy in the workplace could never provide a sound basis for the kind of vibrant shop representation necessary to propagate the union idea and alter management behavior.[16]

Trade union opposition to management's company union gambit also accounts for the Wagner Act's insistence that National Labor Relations Board (NLRB) union certification could not take place in the absence of "majority rule" within a bargaining unit whose jurisdiction was held by one trade union alone. And it explains much of the fixation of the union pioneers upon the seniority principle, designed to curtail management discrimination, as well as their near-obsessive quest for some form of the "union shop," which remained a prime point of contention between labor and capital well into the 1940s. To unionists like John L. Lewis, a veteran and victim of the successful industry counterattack after

World War I, such guarantees of union security were essential to ensure that history would not repeat itself after the next war's employment boom came to an end.

Although these trade union fears of division within and assault from without were well justified, the set of defensive bulwarks they constructed—exclusive jurisdiction, the union shop, elaborate grievance procedures, and a highly centralized form of workplace governance—may well have forestalled a far more flexible and less "adversarial" kind of trade unionism. Today, many in the field of industrial relations advocate a European-style "works council" arrangement in which shop stewards from various unions compose a bargaining council that negotiates with management on a continuous basis. Because such works councils are not part of the union structure itself—they do not bargain over wages, for example—a certain degree of mutual problem solving with lower-level management is possible. But the works council model had no chance in mid-century America. Managers saw shop steward power as a nightmare, subversive of their "prerogatives," and the independent organization of lower-level supervision—a real possibility in the mid-1940s—as tantamount to production anarchy. Meanwhile the unions knew that unless they monopolized the voice of all those they claimed to represent, American managers would not hesitate to encourage the growth of a rival organization designed to subvert the union idea itself.[17]

THE FATE OF POLITICIZED BARGAINING IN THE 1940S

The failure of the trade unions to institutionalize a system of politically structured collective bargaining characteristic of the late 1930s and early 1940s gave rise to what some observers now fondly remember as a labor-management "accord" that governed industrial relations from 1947 to 1978. But the very idea of such a harmonious accord is a suspect reinterpretation of that industrial era. In the first decade after World War II few unionists could be found to declare their relationship with corporate America to be particularly agreeable or stable. Indeed, to the extent that such an accord was reached at all, it was less of a mutually satisfactory concordat than a dictate imposed upon an all-too-reluctant labor movement in an era of its political retreat and internal division.

By 1945 the trade unions were almost at their twentieth-century apogee, in terms of both size and political strength. Sumner Slichter counted them "the most powerful economic organizations which the country has ever seen." As a result of their wartime collaboration with the state, virtually all of the core industrial sectors were unionized; just as important, the unions stood on the verge of new organizing frontiers: in the newly industrialized regions of the South, in retail trade, restaurants, and the telephone business, among first-line supervisors and technicians in heavy industry, and even among white-collar employees in banking and insurance.

This new power was by its very nature political, for the New Deal had thoroughly politicized all relations among the union movement, the business community, and the state. The war intensified this trend, advancing the nation toward the kind of labor-backed corporatism that would characterize social policy in Northern Europe and Scandinavia. Corporatism of this sort placed capital-labor relations within a highly centralized governmental context, where representatives of the contending "peak" organizations bargained politically for their respective constituencies.[18]

The premier examples of such corporatist institutions in 1940s America were the War Labor Board (WLB) and its wartime companion, the Office of Price Administration (OPA), administrative regimes that began to reorder wage and price relations within and between industries. The War Labor Board, for example, socialized much of the trade union movement's prewar agenda, thus mandating seniority and grievance systems, vacation pay, night-shift supplements, sick leave, and paid mealtimes as standard "entitlements" for an increasingly large section of the working class. Although the end of the war was certain to limit the scope of WLB and OPA authority, most liberal and labor spokesmen still saw their programmatic reconstitution as the kernel of a postwar "incomes" policy that would rationalize the labor market, set profit and price guidelines, and redistribute income into worker and consumer hands.

Politicized bargaining, both within the Washington corridors of power and without, opened the door to a social democratic

America. At the end of World War II most trade unionists, especially those in the new industrial union wing, saw collective bargaining as but one element of a far broader labor-left agenda that
they thought essential to the success of their social ambitions.
During World War II, the unions had been largely frustrated in
their efforts to win a large voice in the work of the War Production
Board and other government councils that controlled investment
and manpower policy, but such ambitions were given freer rein in
the years just after 1945. Inspired by reformist Catholic social doctrine, many CIO leaders agitated for both a guaranteed annual
wage and a set of industry councils designed to inject a governmental and a union voice into the highest levels of corporate decisionmaking. The Steelworkers wanted the industry to build more
plants, and the United Automobile Workers tried to protect the
market share of independent producers like Hudson, Packard, and
Kaiser. Meanwhile virtually all labor liberals put a tax-funded rise
in the provision for the nation's social safety net near the top of
their political agenda. This was largely embodied in the Murray-
Wagner-Dingle bill, which foresaw a near European level of social
welfare spending for health care and unemployment benefits as
well as old-age pensions under Social Security.[19]

Politicized bargaining of this sort demanded of the trade
unions an organic amalgamation of strike action, organizing activity, and political mobilization. Consequently, 1946 yielded two
decisive examples of such political unionism. Under Walter
Reuther's leadership the UAW struck General Motors for 113 days
in the fall and winter of 1945–46. Reuther called for a 30 percent
increase in wages without a rise in the cost of cars. GM denounced
his demand as un-American and socialist, but in reality Reuther
was seeking to put some backbone into the Truman administration's efforts to sustain price controls and working-class living standards during the crucial demobilization era. To forestall the widely
expected postwar slump, left-Keynesians like Reuther were not
interested in a new round of government spending, the fiscal prescription favored by liberals a half-generation afterward. Instead,
the UAW program, "Purchasing Power for Prosperity," saw the
progressive redistribution of income as the key lever by which
unions and the government might sustain aggregate demand. Or, as
Reuther put it early in 1946, "The fight of the General Motors

workers is a fight to save truly-free enterprise from death at the hands of its self-appointed champions."[20]

That same year witnessed the CIO's celebrated effort to organize the South. Operation Dixie had two goals. First, organizers sought to unionize Southern textiles, eliminate the North-South wage differential, and thereby forestall the massive flight of jobs and capital out of New England. Second, and even more pressing, the CIO saw the unionization of the South as the central element in an assault upon the industrial oligarchy of that region, whose rule, both at home and in Washington, rested upon the disfranchisement of the Southern working class, both black and white. Verily, the link between CIO-style unionism and the mobilization of an increasingly self-confident black movement had become apparent to the political leadership of the white South, whose militant opposition to even the most attenuated New Deal reforms can be dated from the birth of this interracial alliance in the late 1930s. The unions therefore sought to break the power of the "bourbons" by striking at their heartland, the bastions of racial segregation and low-wage labor in the newly proletarianized regions of the deep South. "When Georgia is organized . . . ," predicted one CIO official, "you will find our old friend Gene Talmadge trying to break into the doors of the CIO conventions and tell our people that he has always been misunderstood."[21]

Finally, the union movement sought to make its political weight felt in an independent and aggressive fashion. The United States had no labor party, but both the AFL and the CIO built political machines that gave labor a distinctive, well-defined political profile at both the national and local levels. The unions invented the political action committee in the 1940s; they wanted to "realign" the Democratic Party by purging the Dixiecrats; and they toyed with the idea of building a new, labor-based party. Union membership has had a significant and lasting impact on the pro-Democratic voting patterns of at least one-third of the electorate. Partisan politics in the early postwar era as a result had something of a social democratic flavor. From 1948 until 1964 every Democratic candidate for president launched his campaign with a Labor Day rally in Detroit's Cadillac Square.[22]

But the larger ambitions of the union movement were defeated in the immediate postwar years. The collapse of the Office of Price

Administration in 1946—after a wave of inflationary wage strikes—doomed the corporatist incomes policy and set the stage for the devastating cost-of-living surge that did so much to discredit the regulatory state, turn middle-class opinion against the trade unions, sweep the GOP back into control of the Congress, and end the prospect for an extension of the New Deal in the postwar era. The stalemate in domestic politics was reinforced by the failure of Operation Dixie, which ensured that the political weight of an essentially undemocratic Southern polity would continue to inject a distorting, "Prussian" element into American statecraft. Even as union concentration rose to European levels in the late 1940s, which sustained the weight of a solid liberal-labor bloc within the Democratic Party, the GOP-Dixiecrat alliance in Congress vetoed union and Democratic Party efforts to bolster the American welfare state or defend the Wagner-era labor relations regime. And because of the vital role the South still played in national Democratic Party politics, even those liberals elected from solidly prolabor constituencies were drawn into compromise and coalition with the right. The CIO bargained with the Democratic Party "much as it would with an employer," admitted union political operative Jack Kroll in the early 1950s.[23]

The labor movement therefore found itself on exceedingly difficult terrain after 1947. Backed by a coalition of business conservatives, Southern bourbons, and antilabor ideologues, the new Republican Congress quickly passed the Taft-Hartley Act over President Harry Truman's veto. Elements of this new law had been on the legislative and political agenda since the late 1930s, when the CIO had burst forward as such a profound disturber of the industrial and political status quo. The AFL sought limits on what the older federation saw as the NLRB's industrial union bias; core industrial firms wanted to halt the spread of unionism into the ranks of foreman and first-line supervisor, while companies in construction, transport, and retail sales hated the secondary boycott, which gave union workers the right to aid their colleagues by refusing to work on any goods that were themselves the product of an industrial dispute. The Republican Party, and not a few Democrats, also feared the CIO's innovative political action committee, which had proved to be the dynamo that ensured Roosevelt's 1944 reelection victory. Finally, all conservatives wanted to force the Communists out of the union movement.

Passage of the Taft-Hartley Act proved a milestone, not only for the actual legal restrictions the new law imposed on the trade unions but as a symbol of the shifting relationship between the unions and the state at the dawn of the postwar era. Taft-Hartley's most ideological, best-remembered consequence was the purge of the Communists from official union posts. Whatever their relationship to Soviet Stalinism, the Communists, who led unions with upwards of one million members, did see the labor movement as an essentially political phenomenon. Their elimination, which required a virtual civil war in unions like the UAW, the United Electrical Workers, and National Maritime Union, chilled internal democracy and strengthened those factions of the union body politic that were tilting these institutions toward a stolid parochialism.

By curbing interunion solidarity, purging the radicals, and eliminating supervisory unionism, the Taft-Hartley law helped ghettoize and depoliticize the labor movement. The new labor law codified the union-free status quo in the cotton South and the entrepreneurial Southwest, especially after most states in those regions took advantage of Taft-Hartley to ban the union shop within their borders. Meanwhile the unionization of finance, engineering, insurance, and other private sector service industries proved virtually impossible with the ban on supervisory unionism and the proscription of the secondary boycott, both of which were essential to the organization of retail trade and the food service sector of the economy. The ranks of these "middle-class," white-collar, and service workers would swell over the next few decades, but whatever the cultural and structural obstacles to their organization, the legal straitjacket imposed by Taft-Hartley ensured that the unions reborn in the New Deal would now be consigned for a generation to a roughly static geographic and demographic terrain, an archipelago that skipped from one blue-collar community to another in the Northeast, the Midwest, and the Pacific Coast region.[24]

Taft-Hartley may not have been the "slave-labor" law denounced by CIO and AFL alike, but if it destroyed few unions, it did nonetheless impose a set of constraints that encouraged trade union parochialism and penalized any serious attempt to project a classwide political-economic strategy. To the corporations this was a major, long-sought victory that made certain that union strength would be limited to the oligopolistically structured industries of the industrial heartland. Thus, even the most liberal of the CIO unions found appealing a narrowly focused, defensive brand of private sector collective bargaining. This was made even more manifest in the wake of President Truman's reelection in 1948. Although his victory came in a contest that saw the most class-polarized vote in this century, all of his legislative efforts to advance a postwar New Deal—national health insurance, higher Social Security benefits, repeal of Taft-Hartley—were rejected by the dominant conservative coalition in Congress.

The stage was set for the union-management "accord" that framed industrial relations during the next three decades. At first the unions proved reluctant partners. When General Motors first offered the UAW "cost of living/annual improvement factor" clauses, which would guarantee auto workers protection against inflation and a real annual increase in their standard of living, the union accepted—a "blue plate special," Walter Reuther called it—but without any illusion that such a bargain represented a fulfillment of its larger postwar program. The UAW still fought for price controls and an overall shift in the sociopolitical balance of power: as Reuther put it, "General Motors workers cannot be bribed with the wooden nickels of inflation into withdrawing from the fight against the greedy industrialists and subservient politicians who caused and condoned the price rises which are now undermining the living standards of millions." The union therefore characterized its 1948 contract, the first with a cost of living adjustment clause, as but a "holding action" that would temporarily protect the income of GM workers in the "context of today's economic and political reaction."

However, such ideological opposition was soon put aside. In the political stalemate that followed Truman's reelection, it became clear that no social democratic breakthrough was in the offing, either toward corporatist wage bargaining or an expansion of the welfare state. Meanwhile the cold war onset of what even administration officials described as a "permanent war economy" made certain that inflationary pressures were deeply embedded within the postwar boom. It was in such a context that the UAW and General Motors negotiated a new collective bargaining agreement that decisively reprivatized wage and welfare bargaining in America's most important industry. The five-year UAW-GM contract of May 1950 guaranteed pensions, health insurance, the union shop, and a 20 percent increase in the standard of living of those auto workers who labored under its provisions.

Unionists like UAW president Reuther were now fulsome in their praise, while *Fortune* magazine dubbed the agreement "The Treaty of Detroit." "GM may have paid a billion for peace but it got a bargain," wrote Daniel Bell, himself once a comrade of Reuther's in the Socialist Party. It was the first major industry contract "that unmistakably accepts the existing distribution of income between wages and profits as 'normal' if not 'fair.'. . . It is the first major union contract that explicitly accepts objective economic facts—cost of living and productivity—as determining wages, thus throwing overboard all theories of wages as determined by political power and of profits as 'surplus value.'" By the early 1960s the COLA principle had been incorporated into more than 50 percent of all major union contracts, and in the inflationary 1960s and 1970s it spread even further: to Social Security and military pensions, and to wage determination in some units of the government and the nonunion private sector. This depoliticizing, this privatization of what had been the union movement's larger sociopolitical agenda also extended to the negotiation of a set of pension, vacation, and health benefits that gave to workers within the core, unionized industries a level of social provision not far below that of the social democratic welfare states of Western Europe.[25]

The firm-centered focus that defined this new era of union bargaining was partly offset by what one historian has called the "soft corporatism" of the 1950s and early 1960s. Critical wage and benefit bargains negotiated by the big unions promised to set the "pattern" for less favorably situated workers, thus generating a kind of classwide settlement in the United States that was characteristic of the more formally corporatist industry-labor relationships in Northern Europe. To avoid unionization, managers at IBM, DuPont, TRW, Weirton Steel, and other unorganized firms in the core industrial sector usually tracked the pattern established in automobiles and steelmaking. A kind of quasi-corporatism even structured bargaining relationships in highly competitive industries like trucking, coal, construction, and the airlines, where New Deal efforts at regulatory cartelization had persisted and where the unions themselves had played a decisive role in organizing the employer associations with which they bargained.[26]

This system collapsed sometime in the 1970s. A considerable debate now rages as to the origins and meaning of its downfall. The conventional wisdom holds that the American accord could exist only insofar as the United States remained an insular, continental market; once the globalization of trade internationalized the supply of labor even the strongest unions found it impossible to defend their capacity to "take wages out of competition." The slow decline in the levels of union density that set in after 1953 therefore reflected not so much a waning of union strength in the core industrial sectors but rather the understandable incapacity of the unions to break out of their blue-collar-job ghetto. The complacency of some unionists, notably AFL-CIO president George Meany, who famously remarked that he did not care if the unionized sector of the workforce continued to shrink, was justified insofar as uniform wage patterns were maintained in the remaining well-organized industries. Thus, the really precipitous decline in union power and membership came only in the late 1970s when firms once thought to be natural oligopolies, like those making steel, cars, and construction equipment, suddenly found themselves competing across a new international market with companies whose unit labor costs stood at one-half or less than those of their own.[27]

The internationalization of the labor market in the 1970s did drive a stake through the heart of the soft corporatism that characterized the postwar accord, but this system was already suffering from multiple wounds and maladies. For all its apparent solidity, pattern bargaining in the United States had a remarkably anemic life. It never spread much beyond the oligopolistically structured core industries, and even there it required a strong union that could equalize labor costs in order to make the pattern hold. Where unions were weak, as in electrical products and textiles, or where domestic competition was fierce, as in automotive parts and food processing, wage and benefit guidelines established in Detroit, Pittsburgh, or Chicago were reproduced only imperfectly. In 1947, for instance, retail clerks earned about two-thirds as much as autoworkers, but after the first big inflationary surge of the late 1960s and early 1970s they took home but one-third as much. Even in the unionized auto parts industry only about one-quarter of all companies, employing 40 percent of the workforce, followed the Big Three pattern during the 1950s. When inflation became a chronic problem after 1965, wage inequality within the blue-collar manufacturing sector increased dramatically.[28]

Nor did the corporatized welfare state encompass more than a highly segmented fraction of the American working class. White male workers in stable firms were its chief beneficiaries. Women, whose work careers were often episodic, were far less likely to build up the continuous employment time necessary for a pension or a long vacation. Likewise, African-American and Latino men found that the firm-centered benefit system worked against them because their disproportionately high level of employment in low-wage, marginal firms often deprived them of full access to the social benefits and regular wages characteristic of the core economy. Because so much of the postwar social struggle has taken place at the level of the firm rather than within a broader political arena, the American industrial relations system has reinforced the economy's tendency to construct such segmented and unequal benefit and compensation schemes. This multitiered system of social provision has served to erode solidarity within the working class and has made it difficult to counter claims that welfare spending and the push for social equity are harmful to economic growth. The classic resentment felt by many blue-collar workers toward those on state-supported welfare has at least one root in the system of double taxation the organized working class has borne in the postwar era. Union workers pay to support two welfare systems: their own, funded by an increasingly burdensome "tax" on their total pay periodically renegotiated in the collective bargaining contract, and that of the government, paid for by a tax structure that grew more regressive as the years advanced. In turn, organized labor has come to be perceived (and all too often perceives itself) as a special interest group, whereby its advocacy of welfare state measures that would raise wages and benefits for all workers has taken on an increasingly perfunctory quality.[29]

The relatively decentralized, firm-centered character of the postwar system has generated not flexibility but dysfunctional rigidities within both the office and shop-floor work regime and the world of union governance. In a system of radically unequal wages and private social benefits provision, parochial job control strategies have much appeal to unionized workers. Detailed work rules, rigid seniority structures, and hard bargaining over new technology represented a rational union response, given the inability of the postwar labor movement either to make wages and working conditions more equitable or to offer a broader political response to layoffs and job dislocation caused by technological change. Thus, in 1959, in one of the longest strikes of the postwar era, the United Steelworkers shut down every firm in basic steel in defense of contract clause 2B, which mandated that technological innovations that threatened to reduce staffing in the mills could not take place without prior union approval. Union-management stalemate on this issue would prove devastating to the health of an industry soon to face a wave of imported steel from highly efficient furnaces constructed after the end of World War II.[30]

These firm-centered rigidities extended to the union structure itself. Although the United States has one of the weakest union movements among the industrial democracies, it nevertheless sustains the largest and best-paid stratum of full-time salaried officers in the world. Virtually every local union of more than a few hundred workers supports a paid functionary, while the "internationals" employ large staffs, both of servicing representatives and technical experts, who devote most of their time to the negotiation and administration of the union's numerous contracts. In the United States functionary/worker ratios are something like one in four hundred. The European average is about one full-time officeholder per two thousand unionists. This bureaucratic overhang is a product both of the relatively large burden inherent in the administration of tens of thousands of individual bargaining relationships and of the opportunities for self-aggrandizement that arise in the same context. During the 1950s and 1960s the union "servicing" function meant that, whatever the politics or personalities of those who led individual unions, the time, money, and effort that went into organizing and internal education fell sharply away. And the outright corruption of unions like the Teamsters, Laborers, Longshoremen, and Confectionery Workers can be blamed on the near irresistible temptations union officials faced when given the opportunity to administer health, welfare, and pension funds that mounted into the billions.[31]

Such top-heavy union bureaucracies proved highly resistant to rotation in office, quite as much in the UAW, where the union's adherence to democratic procedure was advertised in an extravagant fashion, as in the Teamsters or the Building Trades, where little pretense was made of such democratic norms either at the national or local levels. Union leaders often defended the need for internal organizational discipline on the grounds that they faced a set of corporate enemies who had never come to terms with the existence of the institutions they led. Trade unions were not analogous to democratically organized voluntary organizations because they were in a state of continual warfare with adversaries who took every opportunity to use divisions within the workforce to subvert them. As Arthur Goldberg, then the Steelworkers' chief counsel, later President Kennedy's secretary of labor, put it in 1958: "Even where the existence and status of a union is unquestioned—as, for example, in the basic steel industry—it is unlike political government in that it cannot legislate by itself on the matters of primary concern to it—wages, hours and working conditions. . . . If there is analogy to political government, the analogy is to a political government [during] a revolution, and which is periodically at war."[32]

Goldberg's understanding of the tenuousness of even such monolithic unions as the million-member Steelworkers turned out to be more accurate than that of industrial relations academics like Clark Kerr and John Dunlop, who thought unions inherently "functional" to modern industry and management. Whatever the virtues of the labor-management accord in the 1950s and 1960s, industrial peace was not one of them. From the late 1940s through the early 1970s strike levels in the United States were at their highest in the twentieth century. In the steel industry alone there were national strikes in 1946, 1949, 1952, 1956, and 1959. If the unions had been reluctant participants in the "accord" of that era, managers were as well, and they became even more so with each passing year. Industrial warfare was continuous on the nonunion frontier: at Kohler, Lone Star Steel, Dan River Mills, General Electric, and in California agriculture. Such firms, feeling squeezed by the moderate inflation built into the postwar accord, provided much of the impulse that put "right-to-work" referenda on the ballot in California, Ohio, and other industrial states during the 1958 elections.[33]

But the stability of the postwar labor-management accord came under even greater attack when the nation's big industrial firms took their first real opportunity—the recession of 1957–59—to launch an aggressive effort to renegotiate the balance of power in industrial relations. In tandem with the Goldwater wing of the Republican Party, management at many core firms now attacked "monopoly unionism," and, in a turn to what was then dubbed the "new look" in industrial relations, began a concerted effort to regain on the shop floor the managerial prerogatives lost two decades before. This counterattack was given heavy ideological reinforcement by the sensational McClellan Committee hearings of that era, whose exposé of Teamster criminality struck a serious blow at the legitimacy of the entire trade union movement. The Landrum-Griffin Act, passed in 1959, did reform internal union governance, but in a fashion that would come to typify the work of such antiunion fronts as the "National Right to Work Committee," it did so only under conditions that further constrained the power of all trade unions.

Goldberg and the union leadership for which he spoke may have held a realistic understanding of the corporate mind-set and the true balance of power in heavy industry, but the union bureaucratization that he defended proved to be a disaster for American labor. In the course of its mid-century heyday, the inability of American trade unionism to accommodate internal debate and rank-and-file insurgency deprived it of those ideological and human resources essential to its own revitalization. Here the legacy of the early cold war expulsion of the Communists crippled the capacity of the unions to tolerate ideologically motivated dissent. The enormous weight of the paid apparat gave the leadership the tools needed to maintain control. As a result, the insurgencies of those years—whether shop-floor movements to resist management's "new look" in the late 1950s, African-American efforts to prod the unions on the civil rights front in the early 1960s, or New Left militancy a few years later—were easily contained. But the price was exceedingly heavy: an enervation of the union structure and an erosion in the legitimacy of the labor movement as a vital part of American democratic politics.[34]

A SECOND CHANCE IN THE 1960S

During the 1960s the unions had their last chance to strengthen the labor-management accord, expand the frontier of American labor along a new racial and regional front, and reverse the slow decline of labor's weight in American politics. During the Kennedy administration a cohort of old New Dealers led by Arthur Goldberg sought to give the now tattering labor-management accord a more explicitly corporatist flavor; meanwhile the trade unions themselves faced the wave of social ferment that characterized the mid-1960s with an equivocation that sharply limited the institutional and political dividends they could win from that extraordinary era of mass protest.

Kennedy administration efforts to strengthen the postwar New Deal directly were carried out on two fronts: the first, a relatively low-key initiative designed to extend unionism and collective bargaining to the public sector, yielded a remarkable success with important lessons for the growth and health of the union movement; the second, a far-higher-profile effort to formalize under government aegis a new labor market/incomes policy, ended as an instructive failure.

On January 17, 1962, President Kennedy signed Executive Order 10988, which legalized collective bargaining between the federal government and its clerical and technical workforce. Such an order had long been on the labor-liberal agenda, and from labor's point of view, it partly compensated for Kennedy's failure to make progress on more pressing issues: an economic stimulus package that would finally pull the nation out of the recession that had lingered since the late 1950s, national civil rights legislation, and manpower training. The order facilitated the growth of public sector unions whose power and autonomy were clearly inferior to those of the Wagner Act model: they could not strike, bargain for wages, or negotiate over the organization or assignment of personnel.

But the law governing public sector unions—many Northern and Western states would soon follow the federal government—avoided many of the conceptual pitfalls inherent in private sector labor law. Because company unions had never been a threat in the public sector and because civil service protections were kept in place, union recognition, jurisdiction, and security issues were of far less import. The law provided that a union could emerge in at least three forms: as the representative for its members only, as the exclusive voice representing all workers in a unit when it had attained a stable membership of more than 10 percent, and as the signatory to an actual bargaining contract in a unit where it had majority support from the employees. Public sector unionism grew rapidly during the next two decades, not because of the militancy or potency of the workers there—although public school teachers would turn out to be a major exception—but because even relatively ineffectual unions had considerable appeal to white-collar workers. Given an environment in which management was both neutral and bureaucratic, public employee unionism appealed to many workers because it served as an effective lobbyist, educator, grievance facilitator, and interpreter of the civil service rules. Over time such government unions tended to take on the characteristics of private sector institutions, especially in the post office, in prisons, and in municipal employment. By 1996 public sector unionism represented about 40 percent of all organized workers.[35]

The impact of Executive Order 10988 would come later, but in 1961 and 1962 emergency repair work on the decade-old labor-management accord seemed of far greater urgency to both Kennedy administration policymakers and industrial union leaders. President Kennedy sought to wage the cold war with vigor, sustaining U.S. diplomatic and military supremacy. He thought defense of the dollar as the world's reserve currency essential to the projection of American power. Given the fixed exchange rates of that era, inflation had to be kept under strict control in order to manage the nation's increasingly difficult balance of payments problem. Kennedy therefore sought to repoliticize wage negotiations in the core industries in order to reach a settlement within a set of guideposts that linked noninflationary wage growth with the aggregate annual productivity increase. Arthur Goldberg established the president's Labor-Management Advisory Committee toward this end, the closest thing to a formally corporatist institution since World War II. His job was to negotiate an "incomes" policy to ensure that the new wage guideposts fixed by the Council of Economic Advisers—eventually set at 3.2 percent—were respected by both labor and capital.[36]

Many of the issues that would later bedevil the U.S. economy and its system of industrial relations were now put on the Kennedy/Johnson labor relations agenda: the threat of international competition, the effort to "manage" new technologies, and the relative distribution of national income between labor and capital. Trade union leaders were quite willing to accommodate themselves to the Kennedy/Goldberg incomes policy if it were part of a more general, corporatist settlement that expanded employment, raised incomes, and forestalled a new round of managerial assaults upon the unions. Despite some internal grumbling, top unionists supported a government-backed "incomes" policy because it institutionalized the status quo: the unions had been shaken by the recent managerial offensive, and they wanted to preserve the existing distribution of income between labor and capital. This would keep U.S. industry competitive in the emerging world market and give the labor-liberal coalition some leverage over managerial pricing and investment decisions.[37]

Much of the early 1960s debate over "automation" also took place within the context of whether management or labor should bear the costs or reap the benefits of the rapid technological change that was characteristic of manufacturing and transport services in this era. There were two union approaches to this issue. Many craft unionists—including those in the railroad brotherhoods, the printing trades, and construction—fought a rearguard battle in which specific job-destroying technologies were either proscribed or accepted in exchange for clear employment guarantees involving either large lump-sum payments or rigid seniority protections. This strategy was often accompanied by an effort to reduce the workweek and curb excessive overtime in order to spread the existing work. Led by the new AFL-CIO president George Meany, an ex-plumber from the Bronx, the labor federation officially endorsed the thirty-five-hour workweek in 1962. Meany and his building-trades allies retained much of their pre–New Deal worldview: they were not Keynesians but saw competition for a limited set of jobs as a fundamental constraint faced by the labor movement.[38]

The social democratic, industrial wing of the union movement saw the "automation" issue as one best resolved through a program of Keynesian stimulation and labor market reforms, not unlike those famously in place in Sweden. Goldberg wanted to strengthen and federalize state employment departments so as to end discrimination, with respect not only to racial bias but also to the inequitable treatment that arose out of regional and occupational blockages. He wanted a more fluid, national market in labor so that patterns set in the high-wage core of the economy spread more easily to the contingent labor force. Goldberg and Reuther understood that it was

not only, or even primarily, racial discrimination that was responsible for black poverty. Reuther contended, "The argument that
unemployment is largely structural is a new version of the old, discredited notion—always useful to an uneasy conscience—that
unemployment is the fault of the unemployed."[39]

Social democrats like Reuther also rejected the shorter workweek because they stood by the belief that Americans in general
and autoworkers in particular were still in real need of more of
the world's basic material goods. (This was a viewpoint shared by
Kennedy as well, who saw proposals for a thirty-five-hour workweek as virtual sabotage in the cold war context.) Reuther's
Keynesian, macroeconomic focus was evident in a celebrated
exchange of the early 1950s. When the auto union leader toured
one of Ford's newly automated engine plants, an executive taunt-
ed him with the remark, "You know, Walter, not one of these
machines pays union dues." To which Reuther shot back, "And not
one of them buys new Ford cars, either."[40]

With Goldberg's backing and Kennedy's interest, the Reutherite
wing of the union movement pushed to introduce elements of a
Swedish-style system into U.S. labor relations. American social
democrats wanted a "technological clearinghouse" to keep track
of trends in automation, and, in order to limit the inflationary pressures that generated so many industrial disputes, labor sought a
"permanent price hearings agency" to counter the "administered
prices" so easily set within the oligopolistic sector of the economy.
Most important, American liberals wanted to reimpose social and
political controls on capital mobility, forestalling its abandonment
of the urban North, while directing new investment toward the
"depressed areas" that Senator Paul Douglas and writer Michael
Harrington had once again made part of the affluent society's social
imagination. These new initiatives were not simply government
spending programs. Rather, the labor-liberal advocates of that era
sought an incremental strengthening of the broad sociopolitical
environment that had sustained the postwar labor-management
accord. Their project was neither exciting nor the fruit of a mass
social movement. However, the cost of their failure to institutionalize such classwide reforms would soon become all too clear.[41]

The failure of the Kennedy-era labor-liberal alliance had two
sources. First, the most powerful corporations wanted no part of a

new corporatist accord. Whatever the consensus reached inside Goldberg's Labor-Management Advisory Committee, it did not extend to the most critical management players. This became dramatically clear in April 1962, when Goldberg's effort to broker a rock-bottom wage-price concordat in the steel industry collapsed in an explosive confrontation between U.S. Steel and the Kennedy White House. The president forced CEO Roger Blough to rescind his company's price hike, but the collapse of the stock market one month later was taken by most in the administration as a warning that any additional confrontation would carry disastrous economic costs. Both the Kennedy and Johnson administrations continued to "jawbone" a set of wage-price guideposts, but from this point on their program of anti-inflationary regulation was divorced from any effort to strengthen the labor-management accord of the early postwar era.[42]

The second source of failure in the early 1960s was of even greater long-range consequence. In the two decades after the end of World War II American liberalism had undergone a profound transformation in which issues of class inequality and the structure of capitalism faded from center stage, except when they seemed to erupt in unpatriotic, radical strikes or selfish craft union power grabs. During the early cold war years most American liberals interpreted the twentieth-century advance of fascism and communism as indicative of the danger posed by mass/class politics. Thus did Reinhold Niebuhr, the Protestant theologian who would have a large influence on post–World War II liberalism, excoriate his fellow progressives for thinking that the distribution of property was a more fundamental cause of social division and conflict than were racial and ethnic differences.[43]

The rise of a dynamic, morally incisive civil rights movement ratified this shift in liberal consciousness. In the months between the Birmingham demonstrations of May 1963 and the March on Washington twelve weeks later, a new social agenda rose to national prominence. Indeed, the summer of 1963 may well be taken as the moment when the discourse of American liberalism shifted decisively out of the New Deal–labor orbit—the very phrase "industrial democracy" now seemed antique—and into a world in which the racial divide colored all politics. The effort to inject a racially (and later a gender-conscious) egalitarianism into the world

of work modeled itself not upon the struggles of the labor movement but upon the strategic vision and tactical legal innovations of
the movement for African-American civil rights.

From the early 1960s onward the most efficacious and legit-
imate defense of American job rights would be found not through
collective initiative, as codified in the Wagner Act and advanced by
the trade unions, but through an individual claim to civil rights
based on a worker's race, gender, age, or another distinct attribute.
From a legislative point of view the decisive moment in this transformation came when, during the great political opening that followed the Birmingham demonstrations of May 1963, legislation
governing fair employment practices was rolled into the 1964 civil
rights law as Title VII. This is usually considered a great victory,
and it surely was, but as part of the civil rights package, "fair
employment" moved out of a world in which employee rights
were seen as part of the tradition guarded by the unions, the Labor
Department, and the old New Dealers and into a realm in which
work rights were defined and legislated on an individual basis.[44]

In a similar fashion, the reform of the labor market and the
rise in wages, long advocated by the unions, came within a highly
racialized context, for the Johnson administration's "war on poverty" targeted the nation's African-American population, who had
been for so long excluded from the social citizenship embodied
within the New Deal system. This racialization of American social
policy was a product both of the Johnson administration's genuine liberalism and of its somewhat cynical efforts to accommodate
on the cheap the costs of its new reformism. Both the unions and
civil rights movement still advanced much the same legislative agenda: A. Philip Randolph's program for the 1963 March on
Washington included a dramatic, prounion reform of the labor
law and a doubling of the minimum wage; and both the trade
unionists and the poverty warriors worked hard to enact the Great
Society initiatives: Medicare and Medicaid, Head Start, Job
Training, and a liberalization of Aid to Families with Dependent
Children. But whatever the character of this legislative alliance,
Johnson administration social programs channeled resources into
training, education, and government job creation programs for
urban blacks. Initiatives of a more structural sort designed to alter
the urban-industrial balance of power, such as repeal of Section

14b of the Taft-Hartley Act, which would have aided unionization efforts in many southern and western states, or the continua-
tion of funding for the radical Community Action Programs that
fought "city hall," were quickly abandoned after they encountered
unexpected political resistance.[45]

Although the mid-1960s turned out to be a lost opportunity in
so many ways, the rights-conscious ideology engendered by the new
social movements of that era seemed to revitalize the union idea,
relegitimizing the union movement among many whites, including
those whose collars were pink, white, and gray. The civil rights movement and its many heirs replicated the social and political dynamics
that had helped the union movement of the 1930s succeed: linking
ethnic consciousness and social citizenship, advancing federal power
against that of entrenched local elites, and creating a new cadre of
ideologically motivated organizers. The years between 1965 and
1974 were an era of remarkable workplace militancy, greater than
any since that of the immediate post–World War II strike wave.

For the first time in a generation the union movement began
to stir in the South and among employees in public and nonprofit
institutions. In textile plants, restaurants, hospitals, and municipal
service, women workers—and African Americans in particular—
provided the backbone for successful organizing campaigns. A
wildcat strike wave in the Postal Service raised wages and institutionalized collective bargaining even in that once author-
itarian/paternal bureaucracy. "Back in the late 1960s,"
remembered one union organizer, "whenever you went into one
plant the first thing you looked to was how many blacks were
there working. . . . And if there were forty blacks you could count
on forty votes." Doris Turner, a leader of the hospital workers,
came to see the linkage between civil rights and union rights:
"Really and truthfully, they were one struggle, just being waged in
different places."[46]

Rights consciousness spread to every social and demographic
segment of society, to just about every interest group and faction. For
a brief moment even the U.S. government acknowledged the desire
for change in the structure of American work life. "All authority in
our society is being challenged," announced a 1973 Department of
Health, Education and Welfare Report, *Work in America*.
"Professional athletes challenge owners, journalists challenge

editors, consumers challenge manufacturers . . . and young blue col-
lar workers, who have grown up in an environment in which equality is called for in all institutions, are demanding the same rights and
expressing the same values as university students." Such rights consciousness even moved up the corporate hierarchy, where white,
middle-aged managers, caught in the job-threatening profit squeeze
of the mid-1970s, challenged the nineteenth-century "employment at
will" doctrine, which had held that employers "may dismiss their
employees at will . . . for good cause, for no cause, or even for cause
morally wrong. . . ."[47]

During the two decades following the civil rights revolution,
the legislative promulgation or judicial affirmation of workplace
rights encompassing the gender, sexual orientation, age, disability,
and parenthood of employees have put a new and expanded conception of social citizenship on the employment agenda. The two
most important pieces of labor legislation in the United States in
recent years have been the Americans with Disabilities Act of 1990
and the Family and Medical Leave Act of 1993. Meanwhile, the
Equal Employment Opportunities Commission (established under
Title VII of the 1964 civil rights law) actually expanded its authority and jurisdiction during the period in which Republican presi-
dents held the White House. Although highly contested, issues that
encompass the hiring, pay, promotion, and layoff of employees are
now subject to governmental review and private litigation to an
extent the union movement could hardly match, even in the heyday
of the Wagner Act. Indeed, the unfolding of a feminist consciousness within the workplace has helped generate laws covering areas
of interpersonal relations and employer-employee contact once
considered exclusively private.[48]

But at the very moment in which this great rights-conscious revolution was being carried forward, the model of collective action
embodied in the Wagner Act was reaching a virtual dead end in legislatures, in the courts, and in the streets. After the early 1970s the
labor movement found itself with few allies during the increasingly
frequent industrial confrontations that so weakened essential elements
of the collective bargaining system, which had sustained the unions for
almost half a century. This disjuncture between the rights revolution
and the unionizing impulse is a remarkable one, and uniquely
American. In Western Europe, in Canada (Quebec especially), and

even in Poland, Spain, South Africa, and South Korea, the rights revolution of "the sixties" (which was sometimes a decade or more
delayed) strengthened social democratic movements and increased
trade union numbers and power.

Although trade union ranks grew by about two million during
the boom years of the 1960s, organized labor failed to revitalize
itself during that opportune moment. The proportion of all
American workers in the unions continued its slow decline, and
union political influence weakened even at the federal level, where
long-sought labor law reforms were defeated in 1965 and 1978,
years during which both the White House and the Congress were
controlled by the Democrats. Why was this the case?

From an institutional and political perspective American trade
unions were at their most conservative and stolid during these
years. The generation of trade unionists who led the unions in the
1960s and 1970s was the same as those who had battled the
Communists in the 1940s, accommodated themselves to the constraints of the cold war and the labor-management accord shortly
thereafter, and solidified an increasingly intimate relationship with
the Democratic Party in the 1950s and 1960s. The AFL-CIO failed
to support either the 1963 March on Washington or the antiwar
mobilizations of the late 1960s, nor did it back the 1972 presidential candidacy of George McGovern, a Democrat but a Vietnam
dove who had inaugurated his political career with a 1948 vote
for Progressive Party presidential candidate Henry Wallace. Even
Walter Reuther's UAW, which funded and patronized both the civil
rights movement and the early New Left, failed to tap their energy
on behalf of its institutional revitalization. On two critical occa-
sions, Walter Reuther's link to the Democratic Party of Lyndon
Johnson put the UAW apparat in opposition to the insurgent forces
of the decade: first in 1964 when the autoworkers' chief conspired
with Democratic Party loyalists to deprive the Mississippi Freedom
Democratic Party of formal recognition at the Democratic
Convention of that year; and then in 1967 and 1968 when Reuther
discredited himself with one of his natural constituencies—that of
the antiwar movement—by his steadfast refusal to repudiate the
president and his war policy.[49]

Equally important, African-American claims to equity within
the union movement advanced slowly, if at all, whether inside the

crypto-racist building trades or in aggressively liberal institutions like the UAW. Craft union leaders saw black demands for jobs and power as but another assault upon the insular, job-hoarding functionality of their organizations, an outlook Richard Nixon would exploit and attack in 1970 when his administration put forward the controversial Philadelphia Plan, which used a strict set of hiring quotas to integrate the insular building trades. In the automobile industry, on the other hand, anyone could get work in a factory, but the distribution and character of the good jobs had been so codified, by contract, seniority, and shop-floor ethnic politics, that African Americans found themselves invariably at a disadvantage during these years. The bloody Detroit race riot of 1967 did not directly challenge the distribution of power and patronage within UAW-organized factories, but it did testify to the gap that seemed to make the institutions of labor irrelevant to the movement for African-American freedom.

But union conservatism was not alone responsible for the failure of the labor movement to take advantage of the new era of rights consciousness. The rights revolution had divided the liberal Democratic community: the trade union reliance upon the procedural mechanisms adjudicated by the NLRB, designed to generate an "industrial democracy" at the work site, seemed to many far less potent and universal than the rights discourse generated by the state's conception of substantive justice and equal protection under the law. Rights claims, moreover, became associated with the "new politics" of feminism, gay liberation, and multicultural diversity, while organized labor seemed to remain part of the old social and cultural order. By advocating state protection as opposed to collective action, American liberals implicitly endorsed the idea, long associated with antiunion conservatism, that the labor movement could not be trusted to protect individual rights. Only the state and its regulatory apparatus could safeguard the individual from social ills such as racial and gender discrimination. The Democrats, in effect, abandoned the idea of collective action.[50]

The Supreme Court's sweepingly restrictive reinterpretation of the entire scope and meaning of collective bargaining compounded the problem by undercutting the potency and appeal of American trade unionism itself. During the very same season in which Congress passed the 1964 civil rights act the Supreme Court—the liberal Warren Court—ruled in the now obscure *Fiberboard* decision that trade unions had no right to bargain over what the courts defined as issues, such as production planning, price schedules, and investment decisions that lie "at the core of entrepreneurial control." In 1980, in *First National Maintenance Corporation*, the Supreme Court further ruled that companies have no obligation to bargain over—or even to provide advance notice of—the closure of part of their operations. The Court's position was that "the harm likely to be done to an employer's need to operate freely in deciding whether to shut down part of his business for purely economic reasons outweighs the incremental benefit that might be gained through the union's participation in making the decision."[51]

Equally important, the courts turned the very idea of the industrial democracy that had once occupied the very heart of the collective bargaining process into an exclusionary principle that exempted unionized workers from many of the statutory rights those same courts (and legislatures) had begun to create or enforce. According to the legal theory codified during these years, collective bargaining represents a form of industrial self-government. Management and labor are like political parties in a parliamentary democracy: each represents its own constituency and, as in a legislature, engages in debate, conflict, and compromise. Under the contract negotiated between the two parties, disputes are peacefully adjudicated through a process of arbitration, to which the federal courts have long given privileged status.

The Supreme Court has elevated private arbitration under collective bargaining to such an exalted status as to have largely removed labor relations from the realm of public affairs, sealing off arbitration and the collective bargaining process from the rebirth of the rights-conscious constitutionalism that has otherwise been such a notable feature of post-1960s American jurisprudence. When statutory employment rights have come into conflict with collectively bargained work rules, the former have been routinely "preempted" under an expansive definition of Section 301 of the Taft-Hartley Act, thus cutting off unionized workers from the potential benefits of the rights-conscious employment laws that were written in the years after 1964. Ironically, this segregation was the product of the Court's most liberal justices, William O. Douglas among them, whose impulse was to defend both collective bargaining and the autonomy of the arbitration system from conservative legislators who wanted to revive another kind of "rights" discourse, including the "right to work," in the interests of antiunion management. This was especially true after the 1957–58 recession, when entrepreneurial employers of the South and West renewed the assault on "monopoly unionism."[52]

To take yet another set of transmutations, the courts ruled, in a series of decisions throughout the 1950s and 1960s, that huge numbers of workers—professionals, supervisors, technicians, security personnel—were for the purposes of labor law not workers at all. In 1974 the Supreme Court held that the NLRA did not cover anyone who had the authority to "formulate and effectuate management policies by expressing and making operative the decisions of the employer." What that decision says, strictly speaking, is that any employee who has the discretion to think on the job, to use discernment in interpreting commands—anyone whose job has not been reduced to mindless routine—is excluded from the Wagner Act framework of representation. All this was formalized in the Court's infamous *Yeshiva* decision of 1980, which ruled that faculty members at a private university were ipso facto "managers" because they operated in a collegial manner and could make effective recommendations to the administration regarding hiring, budgets, teaching load and content, and other policy matters. In a world of work in which a large proportion of all employees were expected to function as loyal members of a professional team and in which complicated jobs requiring the exercise of much independent judgment abounded, the *Yeshiva* decision proscribed collective bargaining in virtually any work setting not characterized by simple drudgery. Moreover, *Yeshiva* generated a catch-22: the more workers win control and participate in decisionmaking at work, the less likely they are to be protected as workers, in which case the forms of participation might well continue, but merely as a mask for managerial control.[53]

CONCESSION BARGAINING: IDEOLOGY AND ECONOMICS

The shift in the content of liberal rhetoric, downplaying the old idea of "industrial democracy" and replacing it with a far greater emphasis on individual rights, represented but one of the shadows under which the union idea had fallen by the late 1970s. Equally important were the economic transformations of that decade, which also helped strip the labor movement of its social legitimacy and functional rationale. The competitive challenge from Germany, Japan, and other masters of technologically advanced manufacturing undermined the key pillar of New Deal–era labor law and politics: trade unions are good for industrial society because they raise wages, not only for union members themselves but also for the entire working population. But now this idea seemed counterproductive, divisive, and vaguely unpatriotic. High wages made American manufacturing uncompetitive. Keynesian programs of economic stimulation, whether through government tax policy or union wage advance, seemed merely to generate inflation and job losses. And since increases in compensation among unionized workers, who still enjoyed cost-of-living protection in the 1970s, far outpaced income growth in the nonunion sector—the union/nonunion wage differential rose from 19 percent to 30 percent in a single decade—American managers found themselves with a new incentive to put wages back into competitive play, especially in the growing list of industries where union and nonunion firms coexisted.[54] Walter Reuther's oft-repeated plea that "unions can only make progress with the community and not against it," which in the 1950s sought to mollify middle-class consumers fearing a wage-price spiral, now proved uncannily farsighted when applied to the fate of the working class itself.[55]

It was therefore only a matter of time before the management demand for lower labor costs—"concession bargaining"—came to halt and then reverse the wage-and-benefit escalator that had long characterized unionized collective bargaining. Significantly, such concessionary wage negotiations first appeared not in the internationally competitive manufacturing industries but in municipal governance, where a mid-1970s fiscal crisis checked much of the growth in social services and trade unionism in New York and other northern cities. The problems the cities faced were twofold: the structural, involving deindustrialization, a stagnant tax base, and the rising costs of infrastructure, education, and welfare; and the cultural/ideological, exemplified by a growing hostility to universally accessible "public goods" like parks, schools, health care, and other social services. (During New York City's fiscal crisis of

1976, the mass-circulation *Daily News* captured this antitax, antiurban ethos in a celebrated headline: "Ford to City: Drop Dead.") In the broader context of political discontent and social distress, high municipal wages were hardly central to the urban dilemma, but they were a convenient, vulnerable, and racially tinged scapegoat, resented both by that growing proportion of the urban working class whose incomes were stagnant and by the newly mobile bourgeoisie who now found the single-class "edge cities" like Tyson's Corner, Virginia, and Fairfield, Connecticut, an easy escape.[56]

Given the fragility of the labor-management accord and the ideological eclipse of the New Deal's high-wage social policy, it was inevitable that concessionary bargaining would soon take a large toll on private sector incomes. This became dramatically clear at the Chrysler Corporation in 1979, when the number-three automaker stood on the verge of bankruptcy. The story of the Chrysler bailout is like a piece of film—in this case it is the New Deal movie—run backward. The players were much the same as forty-five years before: an important corporation in economic difficulties, a politically sophisticated union, and an interventionist Democratic administration that saw the patterns set in the auto industry as the innovative template for many other firms and industries. But in this film version of the old New Deal drama the politics play in reverse, deconstructing the institutional arrangements and social norms that had once sustained the Rooseveltian compact. Prodded by Chrysler's banking creditors, the Carter administration pushed for wage reductions, layoffs, and a squeeze on supplier plants, insisting that such concessions were the quid pro quo for a billion-dollar corporate loan guarantee. Chrysler's Lee Iacocca ratified this bit of regressive social engineering with the declaration: "It's freeze time, boys. I've got plenty of jobs at seventeen dollars an hour; I don't have any at twenty."[57]

The leadership of the UAW campaigned hard and long among its members for both wage reductions and an abandonment of its incremental efforts to win the four-day workweek and eliminate mandatory overtime. In the late 1930s, backed by the then-new Fair Labor Standards Act, unionists like Sidney Hillman and John L. Lewis had placed wage standardization at the top of their social agenda, even when such a program put inefficient producers out of business. But now UAW president Douglas Fraser and other union officials legitimated the firm-centered logic of their corporate adversary. Recycling one of Walter Reuther's social patriotic slogans, Fraser declared that his union now favored "an equality of sacrifice" among management, suppliers, workers, and banks. Executives did take less pay, the suppliers cut their prices, and the banks extended their loans, but this level of sacrifice for the business community had no long-range consequences.[58]

For American workers, on the other hand, the impact of the bailout was disastrous. The UAW did win a seat on the Chrysler board, but for the first time in forty years autoworkers no longer earned the same wages in each of the Big Three auto firms. As the company slashed its payroll and closed many of its older, urban factories, Chrysler employment dropped by 50 percent. Pattern bargaining in the auto industry collapsed, and deunionization swept the auto parts sector. Encouraged a year later by the Reagan administration's spectacular destruction of the Professional Air Traffic Controllers Union, opportunistic managers in other industries soon replicated elements of the Chrysler settlement, and not only in sectors subject to heightened competition from abroad. Inventive personal managers now deployed a whole set of wage structures designed to embed new wage-and-benefit inequalities within the workforce: two-tier wage systems, the establishment of nonunion subsidiaries ("double-breasting"), employee stock-ownership plans, profit sharing, outsourcing, and lump-sum wage bonuses. The Chrysler bailout therefore had a twofold consequence: the concessionary bargaining in what had once been a flagship firm of American industry offered a powerful model that quickly spread to other firms, where blue-collar wages fell; of equal import, the fragmentation of the collective bargaining process implicit in the bailout gave to many union-management relationships a quality not far different from that of Japanese enterprise unionism, in which workers are given powerful incentives to identify their economic well-being with the fate of their own firm and its management.

The trade union defeats that now came in rapid succession were also a consequence of the political isolation that had so marginalized the labor movement by the late 1970s. The unions had few allies and many critics. As Thomas Edsell, Walter Dean Burnham, and Richard Oestreicher have pointed out, the class content of

American liberalism underwent a profound shift in the years after 1968. As a result of both racial polarization in the late 1960s and the enduring cultural and ideological legacy of the Vietnam war, the electoral base of the Democratic Party shifted toward the middle class, while traditional working-class constituencies either defected to the Republicans or, with even more long-range consequence, simply dropped out of politics. In nearly every presidential election since 1968, class differentiation in voting between the major parties has narrowed, and public policy has become increasingly less egalitarian. The electoral lift the Democratic Party received as a result of the Watergate scandal accentuated this recomposition, giving the Democratic legislative majorities of the late 1970s a "neoliberal" cast that owed little to either the organization or the ideas of traditional labor-liberalism.[59]

Labor's political weakness became graphically clear despite Democratic control of the White House and both houses of Congress in the late 1970s. A neoliberal "marketization" of labor relations and economic policy was now in the ascendancy. Pushed forward by Alfred Kahn in the Carter administration and Senator Edward Kennedy in Congress, the sweeping deregulation of the trucking, railroad, and airline industries soon destroyed labor relations stability in the transport sector and cut unionization rates there by a third. The AFL-CIO's defeat in its 1978 effort to win a very modest reform of NLRB union certification procedures, designed to facilitate its organizing activities, proved even more decisive. The legislative politics of this battle demonstrated the fractious character of the Democratic Party, the intensity of opposition to virtually any liberalization of the labor law, and the seismic shift in sentiment among almost all of the large, unionized firms at the core of the manufacturing economy.

As early as 1977 the AFL-CIO's Committee on Political Education asserted that "the 2-1 Democratic majority in the U.S. House is pure illusion." Labor complained that its opponents had picked up "a goodly number of Democratic votes outside the South." These Democratic defections were matched by unexpected and highly political opposition from those industrial firms that had long been advocates of pattern bargaining and stable labor relations. The AFL-CIO contended that any labor law reform that led to unionization among low-wage competitor firms was actually in the immediate interests of those companies that had a substantial history of collective bargaining, but this argument carried little force in the late 1970s. Douglas Fraser captured the import of the shift in big-business sentiment when, in the aftermath of the 1978 defeat of the NLRB reform, he accused his bargaining adversaries of waging a "one-sided class war in this country," thus discarding "the fragile, unwritten compact previously existing during a period of growth and progress."[60]

UNIONS IN THE REAGAN ERA

With the death of George Meany in 1980, his successor, Lane Kirkland, and others at the top of the labor movement recognized that American unions were in a crisis. For the first time in its history the AFL-CIO actually sponsored a mass demonstration, "Solidarity Day," that brought hundreds of thousands of unionists to the Washington Mall in the summer of 1981. (It did so again a decade later.) The AFL-CIO established a study commission whose report, "The Changing Situation of Workers and Their Unions," realistically assessed the failure of the nation's labor law, the potency of employer opposition, and the fragmentary nature of union power. This was a break from the complacency of the Meany era, but the Kirkland leadership wasted many of its limited political resources on a legislative drive to outlaw employer use of permanent replacements during strikes. Such a goal naturally appealed to the leaders of the big industrial unions, who blamed their strike losses on hard-line employer tactics, but the campaign was conceptually flawed because a prohibition on permanent replacement workers would merely give union members the right to return to work under whatever terms and conditions management saw fit to impose. Such an antiscab law would have done little to resolve organized labor's more fundamental problem: the failure to organize new workers even in those sectors of the economy once heavily unionized. In heartland America—at Caterpillar, Greyhound, and Phelps-Dodge—strikebreakers have been plentiful because employers can tap a huge reservoir of the underemployed and underpaid who both covet and resent the high wages of the unionized minority.[61]

If Kirkland could do nothing to stem the antilabor tide, he did manage the union retreat with a certain organizational tidiness. By the end of his regime the AFL-CIO was once again an inclusive "House of Labor." Although the National Educational Association remained independent, the UAW rejoined the AFL-CIO in 1981 after a thirteen-year absence, the Mineworkers returned with a new reform leadership, and the Teamsters again began paying dues in the late 1980s in a vain effort to win some institutional shelter against the government's massive racketeering probe of the union's corrupt top leadership.[62]

Perhaps the most important AFL-CIO reform of the Kirkland era was that which encouraged union mergers designed to streamline the leadership apparat, avoid costly jurisdictional disputes, and generate a sufficient flow of dues to service the membership and organize new workers. Today, most national trade unions are organized on neither craft nor industrial principles. They are instead "general unions" that opportunistically enroll new workers regardless of occupation, employer, or region. Thus, the UAW recruits health insurance clerks and prison guards, the Steelworkers enroll grocery workers, and the Communications Workers negotiate for state and municipal employees.

Although it is tempting to draw analogies between this organizing latitude and that of the pre–World War I Industrial Workers of the World, with its faith in "One Big Union," the implications for democratic governance are of questionable potency. Given the radically divergent interests of such workers and the resulting lack of unity and common purpose in the bargaining process, union democracy and organizational coherence often suffer. This was tragically apparent during the 1985–86 strike of United Food and Commercial Workers (UFCW) Local P-9, which fought a well-mobilized, CIO-style battle against wage concessions at Hormel in Austin, Minnesota. But the packinghouse locals—once among the most militant industrial unions in the old CIO—represented less than 10 percent of the UFCW membership, whose leadership came out of the Retail Clerks International Union in which regional wage disparities, exclusive craft traditions, and membership anomie were the norm. UFCW leaders, never enthusiastic over the P-9 strike, soon denounced it, after which it collapsed amid bitter and sustained recriminations.[63]

As it became clear that the maintenance of high and uniform wages no longer provided an effective rationale for collective bargaining in a post-Keynesian world of highly competitive markets and growing inequality, the union movement found itself undermined not only by a hostile Reagan administration, wage cuts, and mass layoffs but also by its most profound ideological challenge since the reactionary aftermath of the 1920s Red Scare. By the early 1980s the collective bargaining idea was being eclipsed by a new ideological construct, which went by a variety of names, including that of "nonadversarial labor relations," "employee involvement," "team production," and "jointness." "For many years, we paid for hands and legs," explained a General Motors industrial relations official in the mid-1980s. "We were under the Frederick Taylor method of management . . . [but] we need more than that today, we need a great deal more. . . . There is no doubt that the employee knows more about the job than any member of management can ever know, and so the employee must be enrolled in this battle to try and become more and more competitive."[64]

This new managerialism represented yet another challenge to the industrial relations orthodoxy of the New Deal system. The notion that labor and management had fundamentally different interests in the workplace had been central to the New Deal ethos, and hardly limited to those who viewed class struggle as a motive force in world history. In the 1940s and 1950s managers had often analogized the workplace to a well-oiled machine, in which mass production demanded the construction of a quasi-military system of hierarchical control. The common nomenclature of that era described foremen as the factory's "noncommissioned officers" and the workers as the "rank and file." Thus, discipline and hierarchy were built into the production process, generating grievances, conflict, and mass strikes.[65] During the 1950s Clark Kerr spoke for an influential generation of industrial relations intellectuals whose own careers were premised on the notion that adroit mediation and administration could resolve the resultant social tensions. Kerr did not see irrationality, ill will, or antiquated production technology at the core of labor-management disputes. Rather, "organized labor and management are primarily engaged in sharing between themselves what is, at any one moment of time, a largely given amount of income and power. . . . Conflict is essential to survival. The union which is in constant and complete agreement with management has ceased to be a union."[66]

This perspective seemed increasingly dysfunctional after 1970. From a managerial perspective, the sharp productivity falloff that began in 1969 looked particularly alarming when measured against the seemingly superior and more harmonious Japanese production system. American management's long espousal of a forthrightly hierarchical production model came into question. The militant, peculiarly American attachment to "managerial prerogatives" had generated a hugely unproductive layer of lower-level supervisors, a bureaucratic stratum of far greater weight and cost than in Germany or Japan. To compensate for the managerial hard line, unionists defended a set of "work rules," seniority rights, and job classifications designed to generate some sense of order and pre-dictability within a work-site context that could be both arbitrary and authoritarian in its decisionmaking. Finally, managers under-stood that rapid changes in productive technology did require the willing consent of those on the shop floor itself: if high wages, job security, racial hierarchy, and cold war patriotism were less relevant in sustaining a highly productive workplace regime, then other incentives, ideas, social arrangements, and technological structures would have to be found.[67]

Many trade unionists welcomed management's new interest in the reorganization of the work regime. During the 1930s and 1940s union strategy for ameliorating assembly-line tyranny had involved a dual thrust: strengthening the shop steward movement and grievance arbitration system at the base, while at the top, cam-paigning in Congress, among the federal government's regulatory bodies, and at the bargaining table to win for all workers health and safety reforms, apprenticeship standards, pension guarantees, and, during labor's more ambitious moments, some influence over corporate investment decisions and plant location. But both of these avenues toward workplace reform had been blocked by the mid-1970s, the former as a result of the more hostile legal environment and the union movement's own stolid, bureaucratic routinization of the grievance-handling apparatus, and the latter because of the decline of the New Deal labor-liberal political coalition.

Unions like the UAW therefore seized upon management's new interest in work-site cooperation and participation in order to advance labor's historic interest in democratizing the workplace. This was the influential perspective of UAW vice president Irving

Bluestone, himself an old socialist, who hailed the new "quality of work life" programs that flourished in the late 1970s. Writing at a time when the UAW still saw the incorporation of the "Sixties Generation" of rights-conscious workers as vital, Bluestone was emphatic in insisting that such worker-management cooperation schemes were not designed simply with increased productivity in mind but rather would enable workers to "exercise the democratic right to participate in workplace decisions, including job structure and design, job layout, material flow. . . . In the broadest sense it means decision-making as to how the work place will be managed and how the worker will effectively have a voice in being master of the job rather than subservient to it." Some unionists really ran with this idea. In 1988 the UAW's West Coast regional director enthused: "The workers' revolution has finally come to the shop floor. The people who work on the assembly line have taken charge and have the power to make management do their jobs right."[68]

But such presumptive virtues soon became thoroughly interwoven with an ideology that saw the effort to enhance productivity itself as the central theme in the transformation of the work regime. In the early 1980s when unions faced such devastating layoffs and plant closures, many in organized labor themselves adopted the view that U.S. industry could save itself only by a radical reorganization that would enhance productive flexibility to make American workers competitive with their foreign rivals. Labor's "adversarial" relationship to management must cease, while "multiskilling" and team production would eliminate the old, seniority-based work rules and job classifications. Although a precise definition of what actually constitutes a cooperative work regime remains elusive, some scholars estimate that upward of 50 percent of all workplaces incorporate elements of the new system.[69]

The United States has now had nearly twenty years of experience with the new-style industrial relations. What conclusions can be drawn? First, American workers welcome the bundle of ideas that constitute worker/manager cooperation, participation, and job enrichment. The initial response of almost all workers to a participatory reorganization of the work environment is positive. Employees want challenging jobs and a voice in the enterprise regardless of the degree of unionization, level of technology, or

demographic composition of the workforce. But this was as true in
the 1930s, when organization and collective bargaining offered a
road toward these goals, as it is in the 1990s when the New Deal
system is in such an advanced state of decay.

Although the participatory impulse has been heartfelt among
so many workers, the managerial effort to recapture this democratic sensibility holds little promise for the American trade union
movement. All such managerial schemes are resolutely confined
to a single firm, factory, or office. But as Jonas Pontusson and others have shown, long-term productivity and democratic participation require the reorganization of production, social provision,
and financial practices on a far broader basis. Workers are keenly
aware that penalties for failure to cooperate with management are
all too often layoffs, work transfers, and plant closures. Without
the protections offered by a solid welfare state, a broadly engaged
union movement, and a relatively egalitarian wage structure, efforts
to build industrial democracy in a single work site are largely
doomed, for the imbalance of power between workers and managers cannot be ignored no matter how sincere the collaboration or
elaborate the participatory scheme.[70]

But the bulk of the evidence demonstrates that most participation plans are antithetical to the union idea. Their spirit is that of
the manipulative Hawthorne experiments conducted by Elton Mayo
at Western Electric in the late 1920s, where the principles of industrial psychology, human relations, and personnel management were
first combined. Likewise, the elimination of costly supervisory strata, a notable feature of the team production idea, actually returns
workers to the pre–Great Depression era of the working "straw
boss" and incentive pay plans that embedded speedup, labor discipline, and production quotas within the social organization of
the work itself. One close observer has dubbed such modern team
production schemes "management by stress."[71]

Not surprisingly, the managerial advocates of the new industrial relations have been almost uniformly hostile to suggestions
that cooperation within the workplace take place in a context in
which workers regain some elements of a collective voice. Neither
the plant-level works council idea, now spreading throughout continental Europe, nor a proposal for government-mandated health
and safety committees won management support on the ill-fated

Dunlop Commission, nor did American managers prove willing to countenance any legislative innovations that might facilitate union organizing in return for a reform of NLRA Section 8(a)(2), which outlaws company unions. Instead, the TEAM Act that the Republicans are sponsoring in Congress contemplates a straightforward elimination of the sixty-year ban on employer-dominated employee organizations.

A ROAD FORWARD

Union decline, political defeat, and ideological assault constitute the circumstances from which a new labor leadership and a new strategy seem to be coming to the fore. The accession to the AFL-CIO presidency of John Sweeney and his slate represents the most visible change, but his emergence is the product of decades of debate and turmoil. Although one-party regimes control most trade unions, such machines have become increasingly fragile in recent years because the plant closures, lost strikes, and concession bargaining of the 1980s weakened not only the unions but the authority of their top leadership as well. By the end of that decade, a whole new cohort of aggressive local leaders—in the Teamsters, the Auto Workers, the Nurses Association, and the Service Employees International Union—had become a real presence within the union body politic. In some cases it took almost a quarter-century, but the "Sixties Generation" was finally making its voice heard at the union movement's leadership level. Throughout the early 1990s, the AFL-CIO resisted any wide-ranging internal debate, but once the leadership's Clinton-era legislative agenda—a ban on replacement strikers, defeat of NAFTA, Dunlop Commission reforms, and inauguration of universal health insurance—again fell victim to Democratic division and corporate intransigence, even top union leaders demanded the departure of Lane Kirkland and the adoption of a more aggressive posture, in terms of both organizing and political action.

The agenda of the new union leadership is not far different from that of those who revived the labor movement in the 1930s: open the door to the cadres of the left, welcome new immigrants, carve out a distinctive political presence somewhat independent of the Democrats, and, above all, "organize the unorganized." Although labor-law reform remains one of its legislative ambitions, the Sweeney leadership has concluded that a massive, new commitment of union resources to organizing activity cannot await a favorable revision of the law. "Labor must organize without the law," asserts Sweeney, "so that we can later organize under the law."[72] This perspective replicates that of the Progressive-era railroad and steel unions, who violated antiunion injunctions in order to build public support against harsh judicial constraints, as well as that of the industrial unions of the early New Deal, whose conduct of violent, citywide general strikes during the summer of 1934 demonstrated that the immediate alternative to a prounion labor law at the federal level was industrial chaos and civil strife.

The legal wilderness in which unionists now find themselves does have one important virtue: it has made necessary the creative rediscovery of organizing strategies, including community mobilization, plant occupations, and political action, that the Wagner-era labor law had made obsolete or illegal. Given America's pervasive underemployment, unionists recognize that they must organize an entire labor market and not just the set of workers currently employed at any given firm. That is the strategy adopted by an innovative coalition of Los Angeles unions, which have used the research of urban planning scholars at UCLA to focus on the most vulnerable industrial sectors in the city's huge Alameda Corridor, a twenty-two-mile stretch of light manufacturing that is home to the largest single concentration of nonunion blue-collar workers in the nation. "If you organize shop by shop you pull workers into a vacuum," reflected one organizer, "where there are plenty of other workers out there who can replace them. . . . The employer will always feel he can't afford a union wage because his competitors aren't paying one."[73]

Such an undertaking makes highly relevant the legacy of radical unionism and the rich history of community mobilization. If a particular factory gate is no longer the sole focus of the unionizing effort, then organizers must put a greater premium on enlisting the influence and talents of the unemployed, of stay-at-home mothers, and of young people outside the wage labor market. This was precisely the role played by the neighborhood-based unionism of the needle trades in the Progressive era, and by the CIO two decades later, when rent strikes, boycotts, demonstrations by the unemployed, ethnic mobilizations, and political insurgencies generated an organizing culture that permeated every activity and structure of the labor movement.

This approach also conforms to the changing nature of the modern capitalist enterprise itself. The proliferation in subcontracted and outsourced work, the increase in contingent employment, and the rise of the "virtual" corporation have begun to dissolve the once solid boundary between those inside and outside the firm. As a consequence, the Wagner-era legal framework stands as an obstacle to unionization. For more than sixty years the NLRA has assumed that stable bargaining units could be defined and that union certification elections would involve a considerable proportion of the employees in a given business enterprise. But American capitalism has generated a bewildering array of institutions that hardly fit that structure. As a consequence, American unions need to explore a more flexible organizing model, such as those in the building and garment trades, where for almost a century local unions have operated upon a wide variety of principles: craft, ethnic, regional, and industrial. Such locals are not entirely dissimilar to the European works council: they handle the day-to-day grievances, while an overarching "joint board" or "trades council" bargains to establish the general wage level.[74]

From the era of Samuel Gompers and the Knights of Labor forward, American unionists have recognized that organization, bargaining, and political action are indissolubly linked. In 1908 Gompers first declared, "Reward your friends and punish your enemies"; five decades later Walter Reuther was fond of asserting that "labor's victories at the bargaining table are threatened every other year at the ballot box." Such hard-nosed, pragmatic calculation has long been central to labor political action. In order to sustain trade union organization and make progress in economic bargaining, the unions require a supportive political environment. Thus, even the most conservative trade union leaders have not hesitated to throw money and manpower into the electoral effort. With few exceptions the unions have tilted Democratic since 1912; indeed, since the 1940s they have constituted the backbone of the party in most urban industrial states. The AFL-CIO leadership's stepped-up political commitment in the 1996 campaign season lies squarely within this venerable tradition.[75]

But such a pragmatic calculus is not enough, for politics is not simply a question of who gets what in the American political economy. As this review of labor history has tried to indicate, the fate of American labor is linked to the power of the ideas and values that sustain it. A vigorous trade union movement can do much to relegitimate the union idea within the American polity, but a political party is also essential, not only to advance labor's legislative agenda but also to defend the very idea of collective action and working-class solidarity. Today America's two-and-a-half-party system seems frequently comic, but the potential inherent in political action requires respect and attention. In the two centuries since 1789, political parties have been a pillar of the democratic nation-state because they aggregate factions, crystallize ideologies, and generate a compelling vision of social change. Thus, labor-based political parties have been almost universal in the industrial West. They arise out of a logic that compels unionized labor to reach beyond its own ranks and forge alliances with those natural allies that are either unorganized or demobilized. Although the Democratic Party once contained a strong social democratic tendency that linked unionists to a broader liberal constituency, today it fulfills this function in but a pallid and self-contradictory fashion. Given the decay into which America's contemporary political party system has fallen, labor's reassessment of its political options ought to stand near the top of its agenda. At stake is not just public acceptance of the trade union movement but the revitalization of civil society itself.

NOTES

1. Quoted in Steve Fraser, "The Labor Question," in Steve Fraser and Gary Gerstle, *The Rise and Fall of the New Deal Order, 1930–1980* (Princeton, N.J.: Princeton University Press, 1989), p. 55.

2. Lawrence Mishel, Jared Bernstein, and John Schmitt, *The State of Working America, 1996–97,* Economic Policy Institute Series (Armonk, N.Y.: M. E. Sharpe, Inc., 1997), pp. 4–10; Richard Oestreicher, "The Rules of the Game: Class Politics in Twentieth Century America," in Kevin Boyle, ed., *Organized Labor and American Politics* (Albany: State University of New York Press, forthcoming).

3. Theda Skocpol, *Boomerang: Clinton's Health Security Effort and the Turn against Government in U.S. Politics* (New York: W. W. Norton and Co., 1996).

4. John Judis, "False Dawn," *New Republic,* July 29, 1996, pp. 6, 41.

5. Barry Bluestone and Irving Bluestone, *Negotiating the Future: A Labor Perspective on American Business* (New York: Basic Books, 1992); Richard Freeman, ed., *Working Under Different Rules* (New York: Russell Sage Foundation, 1994); A. B. Cochran, III, "We Participate, They Decide: The Real Stakes in Revising Section 8(a)(2) of the National Labor Relations Act," *Berkeley Journal of Employment and Labor Law* 16, no. 2 (1995): 458–519; Jane Slaughter and Ellis Boal, "Unions Slam Dunlop Commission Proposals," *Labor Notes,* February 1995, p. 1.

6. Kenneth Jost, "Labor Movement's Future," *CQ Researcher* 6 (June 28, 1996): 570; John Lippert, "Suppliers and Demands," *In These Times,* July 8, 1996, pp. 26–27.

7. David Gordon, *Fat and Mean: The Corporate Squeeze of Working Americans and the Myth of Managerial "Downsizing"* (New York: Free Press, 1996), pp. 23–32, 61–90; Richard Rothstein, "Toward a More Perfect Union: New Labor's Hard Road," *American Prospect,* May-June 1996, pp. 42–53.

8. The argument is most forcefully advanced by Michael J. Piore and Charles F. Sabel in their 1984 classic, *The Second Industrial Divide: Possibilities for Prosperity* (New York: Basic Books, 1984).

9. Steven Fraser, *Labor Will Rule: Sidney Hillman and the Rise of American Labor* (New York: Free Press, 1991), pp. 327–33; Alan Brinkley, *The End of Reform: New Deal Liberalism in Recession and War* (New York: Alfred A. Knopf, 1995), pp. 31–105.

10. See the essays by David Brody, Howell John Harris, Nelson Lichtenstein, and Joseph McCartin in Nelson Lichtenstein and Howell John Harris, eds., *Industrial Democracy in America: The Ambiguous Promise* (New York: Cambridge University Press, 1993); Education Department, United Auto Workers, "How to Win for the Union," Detroit, 1940.

11. The classic statements are: Louis Hartz, *The Liberal Tradition in America: An Interpretation of American Political Thought since the Revolution* (New York: Harcourt, Brace and Co., 1955); Selig Perlman, *A Theory of the Labor Movement*, repr. ed. (New York: Augustus M. Kelley Publishers, 1966).

12. Gary Gerstle, *Working-Class Americanism: The Politics of Labor in a Textile City, 1914–1960* (New York: Cambridge University Press, 1989), pp. 153–95; Lizabeth Cohen, *Making a New Deal: Industrial Workers in Chicago, 1919–1939* (New York: Cambridge University Press, 1991), pp. 251–89; Michael K. Honey, *Southern Labor and Black Civil Rights: Organizing Memphis Workers, 1929–1955* (Urbana: University of Illinois Press, 1993), pp. 93–213; Margaret Weir et al., eds., *The Politics of Social Policy in the United States* (Princeton, N.J.: Princeton University Press, 1988), pp. 62–98; Oestreicher, "Rules of the Game."

13. Sanford Jacoby, "American Exceptionalism Revisited: The Importance of Management," in Sanford Jacoby, ed., *Masters to Managers: Historical and Comparative Perspectives on American Employers* (New York: Columbia University Press, 1991), pp. 173–200; Ezra Vogel, "Why Businessmen Distrust Their State: The Political Consciousness of American Corporate Executives," *British Journal of Political Science* 8 (1981), pp. 45–78; Colin Gordon, *New Deals; Business, Labor, and Politics in America, 1920–1935* (New York: Cambridge University Press, 1994), pp. 166–203.

14. Among the outstanding books that explore these issues are Alan Brinkley, *Voices of Protest: Huey Long, Father Coughlin, and the Great Depression* (New York: Alfred A. Knopf, 1982); Fraser, *Labor Will Rule*; Joshua B. Freeman, *In Transit: The Transport Workers Union in New York City* (New York: Oxford University Press, 1989); and Peter Friedlander, *The Emergence of a UAW Local, 1936–1939: A Study in Class and Culture* (Pittsburgh: University of Pittsburgh Press, 1975). See also Nelson Lichtenstein, *The Most Dangerous Man in Detroit: Walter Reuther and the Fate of American Labor* (New York: Basic Books, 1995).

15. Steve Babson, *Building the Union: Skilled Workers and Anglo-Gaelic Immigrants in the Rise of the UAW* (New Brunswick, N.J.: Rutgers University Press, 1991), pp. 39–62; Edward P. Thompson, *The Making of the English Working Class* (New York: Vintage Books, 1963), p. 10. For a contrary view that privileges cultural homogeneity, see Cohen, *Making a New Deal*.

16. Melvyn Dubofsky, *The State and Labor in Modern America* (Chapel Hill: University of North Carolina Press, 1994), pp. 107–23; Sanford Jacoby, *Modern Manors: Welfare Capitalism since the New Deal* (Princeton, N.J.: Princeton University Press, 1997), pp. 57–94, 143–92.

17. Sanford Jacoby, "Current Prospects for Employee Representation in the U.S.: Old Wine in New Bottles?" *Journal of Labor Research* 16, no. 3 (Summer 1995); David Brody, "The Breakdown of Labor's Social Contract," *Dissent*, Winter 1992, pp. 32–41; Sanford Jacoby and Anil Verma, "Enterprise Unions in the United States," *Industrial Relations* 31, no. 1 (Winter 1992). To understand how the works council system functions, consider the case of Ford in Germany. The corporation has no recognition agreement with IG Metall, the big metal union. Instead Ford deals directly with its works council on plant problems and only indirectly with IG Metall on pay matters via the employers' federation of which it is a leading member. The works council members all happen to be IG Metall members, but there is nevertheless a creative tension between the council, the national union, and the company.

18. Nelson Lichtenstein, "From Corporatism to Collective Bargaining: Organized Labor and the Eclipse of Social Democracy in the Postwar Era," in Fraser and Gerstle, *Rise and Fall of the New Deal Order*, pp. 122–34; Robert H. Zieger, *The CIO, 1935–55* (Chapel Hill: University of North Carolina, 1995), pp. 141–252 passim; George Lipsitz, *Rainbow at Midnight: Labor and Culture in the 1940s* (Urbana: University of Illinois Press, 1994), pp. 45–68, 99–119.

19. Lichtenstein, "From Corporatism to Collective Bargaining"; Alan Wolfe, *America's Impasse: The Rise and Fall of the Politics of Growth* (New York: Pantheon Books, 1981).

20. Lichtenstein, *Most Dangerous Man in Detroit*, p. 270.

21. Zieger, *CIO*, pp. 227–241; Barbara S. Griffith, *The Crisis of American Labor: Operation Dixie and the Defeat of the CIO* (Philadelphia: Temple University Press, 1988); "Unionized South Will Oust Reaction, Murray Declares," *Wage Earner*, April 12, 1946; Honey, *Southern Labor and Black Civil Rights*; Ira Katznelson, Kim Geiger, and Daniel Kryder, "Limiting Liberalism: The Southern Veto in Congress, 1933–1950," *Political Science Quarterly* 108, no. 2 (Summer 1993): 283–306.

22. Gilbert Gall, *The Politics of Right to Work: The Labor Federation as Special Interest, 1943–1979* (New York: Greenwood Press, 1988), pp. 55–93; David Brody, "The Uses of Power II," *Workers in Industrial America: Essays on the Twentieth Century Struggle* (New York: Oxford University Press, 1981), pp. 215–21; David Plotke, *Building a Democratic Political Order: Reshaping American Liberalism in the 1930s and 1940s* (New York: Cambridge University Press, 1996), pp. 190–226; Kevin Boyle, *The UAW and the Heyday of American Liberalism, 1945–1968* (Ithaca, N.Y.: Cornell University Press, 1995), pp. 35–82.

23. Meg Jacobs, "'How About Some Meat?': The Office of Price Administration, Consumption Politics, and State Building from the Bottom

Up, 1941–1946," *Journal of American History* 84 (December 1997): 910–41; James C. Foster, *The Union Politic: The CIO Political Action Committee* (Columbia: University of Missouri Press, 1975), pp. 108–175, 196–207 (quote on p. 199); Boyle, *The UAW and the Heyday of American Liberalism,* pp. 83–106.

24. Howell Harris, *The Right to Manage: Industrial Relations Policies of American Business in the 1940s* (Madison: University of Wisconsin Press, 1982), pp. 159–175; Nelson Lichtenstein, "'The Man in the Middle': A Social History of Automobile Industry Foremen," in Lichtenstein and Stephen Meyer, *On the Line: Essays in the History of Autowork* (Urbana: University of Illinois Press, 1989), pp. 167–90; Charles T. Joyce, "Union Busters and Front-Line Supervisors: Restricting and Regulating the Use of Supervisory Employees by Management Consultants During Union Representation Election Campaigns," *University of Pennsylvania Law Review* 135 (1987): 493.

25. Lichtenstein, *The Most Dangerous Man in Detroit,* pp. 279–81; Joel Rogers, "In the Shadow of the Law: Institutional Aspects of Postwar U.S. Union Decline," in Christopher Tomlins and Andrew King, eds., *Labor Law in America* (Baltimore: Johns Hopkins University Press, 1992), pp. 283–302.

26. David Stebenne, *Arthur J. Goldberg, New Deal Liberal* (New York: Oxford University Press, 1996), pp. 120–53; Jack Stieber et al., eds., *U.S. Industrial Relations 1950–1980: A Critical Assessment* (Madison, Wis.: Industrial Relations Research Association, 1981), pp. 1–46.

27. See articles by Joel Rogers, "In the Shadow of the Law"; "Divide and Conquer: Further Reflections on the Distinctive Character of American Labor Laws," *Wisconsin Law Review* 1 (1990): 11–147; and "A Strategy for Labor," *Industrial Relations* 34 (July 1995).

28. U.S. Department of Labor, *Handbook of Labor Statistics,* Bulletin 2217 (Washington, D.C.), 1984, pp. 201–3; Harold Levinson, "Pattern Bargaining: A Case Study of the Automobile Workers," *Quarterly Journal of Economics* (Spring 1959): 299.

29. Thomas Byrne Edsall with Mary D. Edsall, *Chain Reaction: The Impact of Race, Rights, and Taxes on American Politics* (New York: W. W. Norton, 1991), pp. 116–53; Beth Stevens, "Blurring the Boundaries: How the Federal Government Has Influenced Welfare Benefits in the Private Sector," *The Politics of Social Policy in the United States,* pp. 123–48.

30. Stebenne, *Arthur J. Goldberg,* pp. 316–51; David Brody, *In Labor's Cause: Main Themes on the History of the American Worker* (New York: Oxford University Press, 1993), pp. 221–45; Glenn W. Perusek and Kent Worcester, eds., *Trade Union Politics: American Unions and Economic Change, 1960s–1990s* (New York: Humanities Press, 1995), pp. 3–56.

31. Kim Moody, *An Injury to All: The Decline of American Unionism* (New York: Routledge, 1988), pp. 41–69, 147–64.

32. Stebenne, *Arthur J. Goldberg,* p. 169.

33. Clark Kerr, *Industrialism and Industrial Man: The Problems of Labour and Management in Economic Growth* (Cambridge, Mass.: Harvard University Press, 1960); Derek Curtis Bok, *Labor and the American Community* (New York: Simon and Schuster, 1970); Gilbert Gall, "Forming Electoral Coalitions: Lessons from Right-to-Work Campaigns," unpublished paper in author's possession.

34. Mike Davis, *Prisoners of the American Dream: Politics and Economics in the History of the U.S. Working Class* (London: Verso Books, 1986), pp. 102–53; Moody, *Injury to All*, pp. 17–40.

35. Irving Bernstein, *Promises Kept: John F. Kennedy's New Frontier* (New York: Oxford University Press, 1991), pp. 215–16.

36. Stebenne, *Arthur J. Goldberg*, pp. 279–315; James Cochrane, "The Johnson Administration: Moral Suasion Goes to War," in Crauford Goodwin, ed., *Exhortation and Controls: The Search for a Wage-Price Policy, 1945–1971* (Washington, D.C.: Brookings Institution, 1975), pp. 199–214.

37. In *Fat and Mean*, the late David Gordon argued that from the early postwar years onward managerial ranks and salary costs swelled rapidly, not because of any turn toward an economy of "symbolic analysts"—the Robert Reich description—but because managers needed a thick layer of supervision to maintain their prerogatives and because the proliferation of the managerial strata was one effective way to push income distribution in a more inequitable direction. Historian David Stebenne arrives at similar conclusions using archival, not econometric, data. See Stebenne, *Arthur J. Goldberg*, pp. 188–232; and Gordon, *Fat and Mean*, pp. 33–60.

38. Robert Zieger, "George Meany," in Melvyn Dubofsky and Warren Van Tine, eds., *Labor Leaders in America* (Urbana: University of Illinois Press, 1987), pp. 324–49.

39. Margaret Weir, *Politics and Jobs: The Boundaries of Employment Policy in the United States* (Princeton, N.J.: Princeton University Press, 1992), pp. 62–83; Gary Mucciaroni, *The Political Failure of Employment Policy, 1945–1982* (Pittsburgh: University of Pittsburgh Press, 1991); Jonas Pontusson, "Labor, Corporatism, and Industrial Policy: The Swedish Case in Comparative Perspective," *Comparative Politics* 6 (January 1991); Gosta Esping-Andersen, *Politics against Markets: The Social Democratic Road to Power* (Princeton, N.J.: Princeton University Press, 1985); Lichtenstein, *Most Dangerous Man in Detroit*, p. 365.

40. Benjamin Kline Hunnicutt, *Work without End: Abandoning Shorter Hours for the Right to Work* (Philadelphia: Temple University Press, 1988), pp. 320–40; Juliet B. Schor, *The Overworked American: The Unexpected Decline of Leisure* (New York: Basic Books, 1991), pp. 122–38; Lichtenstein, *Most Dangerous Man in Detroit*, p. 291.

41. Boyle, *UAW and the Heyday of American Liberalism*, pp. 132–60; Steven Amberg, *Labor and the Postwar Political Economy* (Philadelphia: Temple University Press, 1992), pp. 228–74.

42. Stebenne, *Arthur J. Goldberg*, pp. 253–304; Bernstein, *Promises Kept*, pp. 133–57.

43. Gary Gerstle, "The Protean Character of American Liberalism," *American Historical Review* 99 (October 1994): 1070; Alan Brinkley, *The End of Reform: New Deal Liberalism in Recession and War* (New York: Alfed A. Knopf, 1995), pp. 201–64.

44. An excellent discussion of this sea change is found in Judith Stein, "African-Americans and Labor Legislation in the 1960s" (unpublished paper delivered at the George Meany Center, November 1994); see also Paula F. Pfeffer, *A. Philip Randolph, Pioneer of the Civil Rights Movement* (Baton Rouge: Louisiana State University Press, 1990), pp. 190–95.

45. Weir, *Politics and Jobs*, pp. 83–110; Ira Katznelson, "Was the Great Society a Lost Opportunity?" in Fraser and Gerstle, *Rise and Fall of the New Deal Order*, pp. 185–211.

46. Joshua Freeman et al., *Who Built America? Working People and the Nation's Economy, Politics, Culture, and Society: From the Golden Age to the Present* (New York: Pantheon, 1992), pp. 586–604; Leon Fink and Brian Greenberg, *Upheaval in the Quiet Zone: A History of Hospital Workers' Union, Local 1199* (Urbana: University of Illinois Press, 1989), p. 113; Moody, *Injury to All*, pp. 249–70.

47. U.S. Department of Health, Education and Welfare, *Work in America: Report of a Special Task Force to the Secretary of Health, Education and Welfare* (Cambridge, Mass.: MIT Press, 1971), p. 49; Charles C. Heckscher, "Crisis and Opportunity for Labor," *Labor Law Journal* 38 (August 1987); see also Charles C. Heckscher, *The New Unionism: Employee Involvement in the Changing Corporation* (New York: Basic Books, 1988).

48. The most encyclopedic account of the EEOC is Hugh Davis Graham, *The Civil Rights Era: Origins and Development of National Policy, 1960–1972* (New York: Oxford University Press, 1990).

49. I discuss these developments in *The Most Dangerous Man in Detroit*, but accounts can also be found in Boyle, *UAW and the Heyday of American Liberalism*; and Todd Gitlin, *The Sixties: Years of Hope, Days of Rage* (New York: Bantam Books, 1987).

50. Ruth O'Brien, "Duality and Division: The Development of American Labour Policy from the Wagner Act to the Civil Rights Act," *International Contributions to Labour Studies* 4 (1994): 21–51.

51. James B. Atleson, *Values and Assumptions in American Labor Law* (Amherst: University of Massachussets Press, 1983), pp. 124–30; Paul C. Weiler, *Governing the Workplace: The Future of Labor and Employment Law* (Cambridge, Mass.: Harvard University Press, 1990), pp. 7–47.

52. Katherine Stone, "The Legacy of Industrial Pluralism: The Tension between Individual Employment Rights and the New Deal Collective Bargaining System," *University of Chicago Law Review* 59 (1992): 575; see also David Abraham, "Individual Autonomy and Collective Empowerment in Labor Law: Union Membership Resignations and

Strikebreaking in the New Economy," *New York University Law Review* 63 (1988): 1268.

53. Karl E. Klare, "The Bitter and the Sweet: Reflections on the Supreme Court's *Yeshiva* Decision," *Socialist Review* 99 (September-October 1983); James Begin and Barbara Lee, "NLRA Exclusion Criteria and Professional Work," *Industrial Relations* 26 (Winter 1987): 83–95.

54. Gordon, *Fat and Mean*, p. 221; Joel Rogers, "Strategy for Labor."

55. Lichtenstein, *Most Dangerous Man in Detroit*, pp. 442–43.

56. Studies of the 1970s urban fiscal crisis include Robert Kuttner, *Revolt of the Haves: Taxpayer Revolts and the Politics of Austerity* (New York: Simon and Schuster, 1980); and David Mermelstein and Roger Alcaly, eds., *The Fiscal Crisis of American Cities: Essays on the Political Economy of Urban America with Special Reference to New York* (New York: Vintage Books, 1977).

57. Robert B. Reich and John D. Donahue, *New Deals: The Chrysler Revival and the American System* (New York: Times Books, 1985), p. 126.

58. Moody, *Injury to All*, pp. 165–91; Harry C. Katz, *Shifting Gears: Changing Labor Relations in the U.S. Automobile Industry* (Cambridge: MIT Press, 1985), pp. 51–58.

59. Thomas Byrne Edsall, *The New Politics of Inequality* (New York: W. W. Norton and Co., 1984), pp. 23–66; Kevin Phillips, *The Politics of Rich and Poor: Wealth and the American Electorate in the Reagan Aftermath* (New York: Random House, 1990), pp. 32–53; Robert Kuttner, *The Life of the Party: Democratic Prospects in 1988 and Beyond* (New York: Penguin Books, 1987), pp. 1–33, 72–109; Thomas Ferguson and Joel Rogers, *Right Turn: The Decline of the Democrats and the Future of American Politics* (New York: Hill and Wang, 1986), pp. 78–161.

60. Moody, *Injury to All*, pp. 146–48; Gary Fink, "Labor Law Reform during the Carter Administration: An Opportunity Missed?" in Boyle, *American Unions and National Politics*.

61. AFL-CIO, *The Changing Situation of Workers and Their Unions* (Washington, D.C.: AFL-CIO, 1985); Richard Rothstein, "Toward a More Perfect Union," *American Prospect*, May-June 1996, p. 48.

62. The history of these union disaffiliations is complex. The NEA, which began as a professional association of teachers and administrators, evolved into a genuine trade union, but it never joined the AFL-CIO because a merger could not be worked out with the American Federation of Teachers. John L. Lewis had pulled the UMW out of the AFL in 1947 in a dispute over compliance with the Taft-Hartley Act, and Walter Reuther had broken with George Meany's AFL-CIO in 1968 in a vain effort to set up a new and more dynamic labor federation. Meanwhile the Teamsters had been expelled from the AFL-CIO in 1958 because Jimmy Hoffa and his associates had become such high-profile symbols of union corruption. Much of this is covered in Robert H. Zieger, *American Workers, American Unions* (Baltimore: Johns Hopkins University Press, 1994).

63. Moody, *Injury to All*, pp. 196–98.

64. As quoted in Mike Parker, "Industrial Relations Myth and Shop-floor Reality," in Lichtenstein and Harris, *Industrial Democracy in America*, p. 255.

65. Harris, *Right to Manage*, pp. 99–123; see also Stephen P. Waring, *Taylorism Transformed: Scientific Management Theory since 1945* (Chapel Hill: University of North Carolina Press, 1991).

66. Clark Kerr, "Industrial Conflict and Its Mediation," in his *Labor and Management in Industrial Society* (New York: Anchor Books, 1964), pp. 169–70.

67. Waring, *Taylorism Transformed*, pp. 132–59; Piore and Sabel, *Second Industrial Divide* pp. 251–308.

68. Irving Bluestone, "Human Dignity Is What It's All About," *Viewpoint*, AFL-CIO Industrial Union Department, Washington, D.C. 1978; Bruce Lee, "Worker Harmony Makes NUMMI Work," *New York Times*, December 25, 1988.

69. Thomas A. Kochan and Paul Osterman, *The Mutual Gains Enterprise: Forging a Winning Partnership among Labor, Management, and Government* (Boston: Harvard Business School Press, 1994), pp. 79–109; Bluestone and Bluestone, *Negotiating the Future*, pp. 189–246.

70. Jonas Pontusson, "Unions, New Technology, and Job Redesign at Volvo and British Leyland," in Miriam Golden and Jonas Pontusson, eds., *Bargaining for Change: Union Politics in North America and Europe* (Ithaca, N.Y.: Cornell University Press, 1992), pp. 277–306; Parker, "Industrial Relations Myth and Shop-floor Reality," pp. 249–74; Ruth Milkman, "Labor and Management in Uncertain Times," in Alan Wolfe, ed., *America at Century's End* (Berkeley: University of California Press, 1991), pp. 131–51.

71. Richard Gillespie, Louis Galambas, and Robert Gallman, eds., *Manufacturing Knowledge: A History of the Hawthorne Experiments* (New York: Cambridge University Press, 1991); Nelson Lichtenstein, "The Union's Early Days: Shop Stewards and Seniority Rights," in Mike Parker and Jane Slaughter, *Choosing Sides: Unions and the Team Concept* (Boston: South End Press, 1988), pp. 65–73; Parker, "Industrial Relations Myth and Shop-floor Reality."

72. John J. Sweeney and David Kusnet, *America Needs a Raise: Fighting for Economic Security and Social Justice* (Boston: Houghton Mifflin, 1996).

73. William Forbath and Jon Sawyer, "Will Labor Rise Again? History in the Future Tense," unpublished paper in author's possession.

74. Howard Wial, "New Bargaining Structures for New Forms of Business Organization," paper prepared for delivery, AFL-CIO/Cornell University Conference on Labor Law Reform, October 24–26, 1995; Steve Early, "Membership-based Organizing vs. the Mobile Organizer Model: Worker Empowerment Is the Way to Win," unpublished paper in author's possession; Forbath and Sawyer, "Will Labor Rise Again?"; Dorothy Sue Cobble, *Dishing it Out: Waitresses and Their Unions in the Twentieth Century* (Urbana: University of Illinois Press, 1991).

75. Julie Greene, *Pure and Simple Politics: The American Federation of Labor, 1881 to 1917* (New York: Cambridge University Press, 1998), pp. 142–214 passim; Lichtenstein, *Most Dangerous Man in Detroit*, pp. 350–53; Joseph C. Goulden, *Meany: The Unchallenged Strong Man of American Labor* (New York: Atheneum, 1972), pp. 404–29.

Index

Accord, labor-management, 76–78; attempts to revitalize, 82–84, 86–87; challenges to, 81–82; collapse in auto industry, 97; rigidities generated by, 79–80; strikes during, 81

AFL. *See* American Federation of Labor

AFL-CIO: 1978 defeat of NLRB reform effort, 98–99; 1996 political commitment of, 107–108; aggressive organizing by, 49; conservatism in (1960s–1970s), 91; globalization and, 46; under Kirkland, 99–100; mass demonstrations sponsored by, 99; new leadership of, 37, 38; relations with other unions, 100, 115*n*62; revitalization of, changes required for, 44; under Sweeney, 38, 105–106; and union democracy, 51

African Americans: employment-rights movements of, 54; firm-centered benefit system and, 79; and labor movement, 89, 91–92; meaning of unionism for, 66; war on poverty and, 88

Agriculture, union-member versus nonmember wages in, 9

American Federation of Labor (AFL): composition of, 67; rivalry with CIO, 67, 68; *See also* AFL-CIO

Americans with Disabilities Act (1990), 54, 90

Automobile industry: 1979 Chrysler bailout and, 96–97; decline in union participation in, 62; globalization and transformations in, 50; racial

---

Note: Page numbers in *italics* indicate material presented in figures, tables, and boxes. Page numbers followed by letter *n* refer to notes.